Fodor's InFocus

ARUBA

2nd Edition

Fodor's Travel Publications   New York, Toronto, London, Sydney, Auckland

www.fodors.com

Be a Fodor's Correspondent

Your opinion matters. It matters to us. It matters to your fellow Fodor's travelers, too. And we'd like to hear it. In fact, we *need* to hear it. When you share your experiences and opinions, you become an active member of the Fodor's community. Here's how you can help improve Fodor's for all of us.

Tell us when we're right. We rely on local writers to give you an insider's perspective. But our writers and staff editors also depend on you. Your positive feedback is a vote to renew our recommendations for the next edition.

Tell us when we're wrong. We update most of our guides every year. But things change. If any of our descriptions are inaccurate or inadequate, we'll incorporate your changes in the next edition and will correct factual errors at fodors.com *immediately*.

Tell us what to include. You probably have had fantastic travel experiences that aren't yet in Fodor's. Why not share them with a community of like-minded travelers? Share your discoveries and experiences with everyone directly at fodors.com. Your input may lead us to add a new listing or a higher recommendation.

Give us your opinion instantly at our feedback center at www.fodors.com/feedback. You may also e-mail editors@fodors.com with the subject line "In Focus Aruba Editor." Or send your nominations, comments, and complaints by mail to In Focus Aruba Editor, Fodor's, 1745 Broadway, New York, NY 10019.

Happy Traveling!

Tim Jarrell, Publisher

FODOR'S IN FOCUS ARUBA

Series editor: Douglas Stallings

Editor: Douglas Stallings
Writer: Vernon O'Reilly Ramesar

Production Editor: Astrid deRidder

Maps & Illustrations: David Lindroth, Ed Jacobus, William Wu, with additional cartography provided by Henry Columb, Mark Stroud, and Ali Baird, Moon Street Cartography; *cartographers*; Bob Blake and Rebecca Baer, *map editors;* William Wu, *information graphics*

Design: Fabrizio La Rocca, *creative director*; Guido Caroti, *art director*; Ann McBride, *designer*; Melanie Marin, *senior picture editor*

Cover Photo: Divi Divi Tree, Aruba: Tom Mackie/Alamy

Production Manager: Amanda Bullock

2nd Edition

ISBN 978–1–4000–0873–5
ISSN 1939–988X

SPECIAL SALES

This book is available for special discounts for bulk purchases for sales promotions or premiums. Special editions, including personalized covers, excerpts of existing books, and corporate imprints, can be created in large quantities for special needs. For more information, write to Special Markets/Premium Sales, 1745 Broadway, MD 6-2, New York, New York, NY 10019, or e-mail specialmarkets@randomhouse.com.

AN IMPORTANT TIP & AN INVITATION

Although all prices, opening times, and other details in this book are based on information supplied to us at press time, changes occur all the time in the travel world, and Fodor's cannot accept responsibility for facts that become outdated or for inadvertent errors or omissions. **So always confirm information when it matters,** especially if you're making a detour to visit a specific place. Your experiences—positive and negative—matter to us. If we have missed or misstated something, **please write to us.** We follow up on all suggestions. Contact the In Focus Aruba editor at editors@fodors.com or c/o Fodor's at 1745 Broadway, New York, NY 10019.

PRINTED IN CHINA
10 9 8 7 6 5 4 3 2

CONTENTS

DID YOU KNOW?

Aruba's waters are exceptionally clear, especially on the leeward side of the island, where underwater visibility can be up to 90 feet.

ABOUT THIS BOOK

Our Ratings

We wouldn't recommend a place that wasn't worth your time, but sometimes a place is so experiential that superlatives don't do it justice. These sights and properties get our highest rating, **Fodor's Choice**, indicated by orange stars throughout this book. Black stars highlight places we deem **Highly Recommended** places that our writers, editors, and readers praise again and again for consistency and excellence. Care to nominate a place or suggest that we rate one more highly? Visit our feedback center at www.fodors.com/feedback.

Budget Well

Want to pay with plastic? **AE, D, DC, MC, V** following restaurant and hotel listings indicate if American Express, Discover, Diners Club, MasterCard, and Visa are accepted.

Restaurants

Unless we state otherwise, restaurants are open for lunch and dinner daily. We mention dress only when there's a specific requirement and reservations only when they're essential or not accepted—it's always best to book ahead.

Hotels

Hotels have private bath, phone, TV, and air-conditioning and operate on the European Plan (aka EP, meaning without meals), unless we specify otherwise.

Many Listings
- ★ Fodor's Choice
- ★ Highly recommended
- ⊠ Physical address
- ✛ Directions
- ⌖ Mailing address
- ☏ Telephone
- 🖷 Fax
- ⊕ On the Web
- ✉ E-mail
- 🎟 Admission fee
- ⊗ Open/closed times
- Ⓜ Metro stations
- ⊟ Credit cards

Hotels & Restaurants
- 🏨 Hotel
- ⌗ Number of rooms
- ⚫ Facilities
- ⼌ Meal plans
- ✕ Restaurant
- ⌕ Reservations
- ⍉ Smoking
- 🍷 BYOB
- ✕🏨 Hotel with restaurant that warrants a visit

Outdoors
- ⛳ Golf
- ⛺ Camping

Other
- ☾ Family-friendly
- ⇨ See also
- ⊠ Branch address
- ☞ Take note

Experience
Aruba

1

WHAT'S WHERE

1 Palm Beach. Aruba's biggest high-rise hotels are located along Palm Beach, which is one of the island's best swimming beaches, with calm water. You'll have your widest choice of big resorts, restaurants, casinos, and water sports here, but this is a busy place, so don't go here to escape from the crowds.

2 Eagle Beach. Aruba's so-called "low-rise" hotel area is lined with smaller boutique resorts but also, increasingly, timeshare resorts. Still, Eagle Beach is wider than Palm Beach, so it's not as crowded, and it's the island's best big beach.

3 Manchebo Beach. Just south of Eagle Beach, Manchebo has rougher surf, but it's rarely as crowded and has many fewer resorts. The beach here flows directly into Druif Beach, which is dominated by the sprawling Divi resort complex.

4 Oranjestad. Aruba's capital is a great place to go for shopping, restaurants, and nightlife or to make arrangements for a tour or other activity. Although there are a few hotels here, including the beautiful Renaissance Aruba, the city has no beachfront.

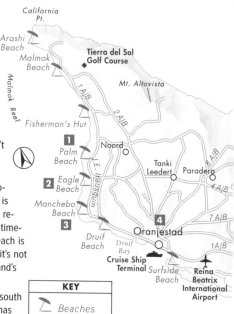

California Pt.

Arashi Beach

Malmok Beach

Malmok Reef

Tierra del Sol Golf Course

Mt. Altovista

Fisherman's Hut

1 A/B   2 A/B

1 Palm Beach

Noord

Tanki Leendert

Paradera

6 A/B

4 A/B

2 Eagle Beach

J.E. Irausquin

Manchebo Beach

3

Druif Beach

4 Oranjestad

7 A/B

Druif Bay

Cruise Ship Terminal   Surfside Beach

1A/B

Reina Beatrix International Airport

KEY
⤢ Beaches

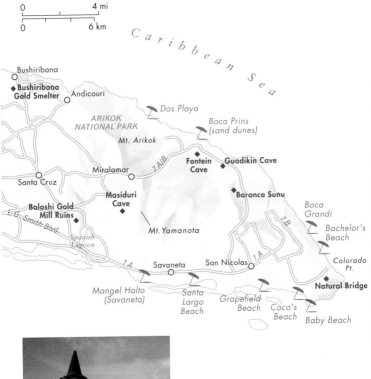

EXPERIENCE ARUBA PLANNER

Island Activities	Logistics

Island Activities

Since soft, sandy **beaches** and turquoise waters are the biggest draws in Aruba, they can be crowded. Eagle Beach is the best the island has to offer.

Aruba also comes alive by night, and has become a true **party hot spot**. The casinos—though not as elaborate as those in Las Vegas—are among the best of any Caribbean island.

Restaurants are very good, though sometimes expensive.

Diving is good in Aruba, though perhaps not as great as in Bonaire.

Near-constant breezes and tranquil, protected waters have proven to be a boon for **windsurfers,** who have discovered that conditions on the southwestern coast are ideal for their sport.

A largely undeveloped region in Arikok National Wildlife Park is the destination of choice for visitors wishing to **hike** and explore some wild terrain.

Logistics

Getting to Aruba: Aruba is 2½ hours from Miami and 4½ hours from New York. Smaller airlines connect the Dutch islands in the Caribbean, often using Aruba as a hub. Travelers to the U.S. clear Customs and Immigration before leaving Aruba.

Nonstops: There are nonstop flights from Atlanta (Delta), Boston (American, JetBlue, US Airways), Charlotte (US Airways), Chicago (United—weekly), Fort Lauderdale (Spirit—weekly), Houston (Continental—twice-weekly), Miami (American), Newark (Continental), New York–JFK (American, Delta, JetBlue), New York–LGA (Continental—weekly), Philadelphia (US Airways—twice-weekly), and Washington, DC–Dulles (United), though not all flights are daily.

On the Ground

A taxi from the airport to most hotels takes about 20 minutes. It will cost about $17 to get to the hotels along Eagle Beach, $20 to the high-rise hotels on Palm Beach, and $10 to the hotels downtown. Buses are also an option for traveling around the island, and are especially convenient for shorter trips. Buses only run once an hour, but the price is right, at $1.25 one-way ($2.25 round-trip).

Renting a Car: Rent a car to explore independently, but for just getting to and around town taxis are preferable, and you can use tour companies to arrange your activities. Rent a four-wheel-drive vehicle if you plan to explore the island's natural sights.

Dining and Lodging on Aruba

Aruba is known for its large, luxurious high-rise resorts and vast array of time-shares. But the island also has a nice selection of smaller, low-rise resorts for travelers who do not want to feel lost in a large, impersonal hotel complex. If you are on a budget, consider booking one of the island's many apartment-style units, so you can eat in sometimes instead of having to rely on restaurants exclusively.

Since the all-inclusive resort scheme has not taken over Aruba, as it has many other islands, you'll find a wide range of good independent and resort-based restaurant choices. There is a variety of restaurants in Oranjestad, the island's capital, but you'll also find good choices in the resort areas of Eagle and Palm Beach, as well as Savaneta and San Nicolas.

Hotel and Restaurant Costs

Restaurant prices are for a main course at dinner, and include any taxes or service charges. Hotel prices are per night for a double room in high season, excluding taxes, service charges, and meal plans (except at all-inclusives).

Tips for Travelers

Traffic into and out of Oranjestad can be heavy during rush hour. Allow a bit of extra time if you are trying to get into town for dinner.

Aruba is renowned for its nightlife and casinos, and the legal drinking and gambling age is 18.

You can safely drink the water in Aruba, but you may not want to. Almost all of the island's water is desalinzed seawater, and you may not like the taste.

Electricity in Aruba is 110 volts, just like in the U.S.

You probably will not need to change any money if you are coming from the U.S. American currency is accepted almost everywhere in Aruba, though you might get some change back in local currency.

What It Costs in U.S. Dollars

	$$$$	$$$	$$	$	¢
Restaurants	over $30	$20–$30	$12–$20	$8–$12	under $8
Hotels*	over $350	$250–$350	$150–$250	$80–$150	under $80
Hotels**	over $450	$350–$450	$250–$350	$125–$250	under $125

* Indicates hotels on the European Plan (EP—no meals), Continental Plan (CP—with a continental breakfast), or Breakfast Plan (BP—with full breakfast), ** Indicates hotels on the Modified American Plan (MAP—with breakfast and dinner), Full American Plan (FAP—including all meals but no drinks), or All-Inclusive (AI—with all meals, drinks, and most activities).

TOP EXPERIENCES

Diving below the sea

(A) True, the diving around Aruba is not quite as spectacular as in nearby Bonaire, but with visibility as high as 90 feet and with most of the best and most popular dive sites in waters only 30 to 60 feet deep, Aruba offers an ideal diving environment for both the experienced and novice diver. The healthy coral reefs draw a multitude of fish. Seek out one of the island's experienced dive operators, such as Aruba Pro Dive, to show you where to go.

The joy of snorkeling

(B) You don't have to be a certified diver to experience the island's underwater beauty. Snorkeling is easy and a must in Aruba, either by yourself or on a snorkel cruise. Wherever you duck under, you'll be inducted into a mesmerizing world underwater. Slow down and keep your eyes open: even fish dressed in camouflage can be spotted when they snatch at food passing by. The placid waters of Baby Beach offeres a good reef close to shore.

Dinner at Madame Janette's

(C) You may have a close encounter with the ghost of Auguste Escoffier at the island's most elegant and exquisite restaurant; expect classic Continental food, but if you are looking for something a bit more traditional, you'll find no better in Aruba. By the way, there's no "madame" here, unless you want to pay homage to the fiery Scotch bonnet pepper sauce for which the restaurant is named.

Bar-hopping on the Kukoo Kunuku

(D) For those who want to maximize their bar-hopping capabilities but minimize the necessity for

driving, the Kukoo Kunuku may be just the ticket. The bus, a psychedelically painted 1957 Chevy bus, is party central for up to 40 people nightly. Reserve your place in advance, and the bus will pick you up (and pour you out) at your hotel, saving a chance encounter with the local drunk-driving police.

Relaxing on Eagle Beach

(E) The best beach on Aruba (if not in the entire Caribbean's), Eagle Beach is wide, soft, and beautiful. Though now lined with time-shares and other resorts, the mile-long beauty has grown even wider since 2004 after a couple of hurricanes.

Partying at the Bon Bini Festival

Bon Bini means welcome in Papiamento, the language of Aruba. This weekly festival is held every Tuesday evening at Fort Zoutman in Oranjestad. For a small fee you get to listen to a local steel-pan band, sample local food and drink, and get a sense of what Aruban culture has to offer.

Dining on the sands at Passions

Every night the Amsterdam Manor Beach Resort turns its beachfront into Passions, a romantic on-the-beach restaurant lit by tiki torches. Excellent cuisine is served along with great cocktails as you dine just inches from the lapping waves.

Cooling off at one of Aruba's low-rise resorts

Aruba is not all high-rises and frenetic activity. The island also has some fine, family-owned boutique resorts. Most of these, including Amsterdam Manor Beach Resort and Bucuti Beach Resort (two of Aruba's finest), can be found right

TOP EXPERIENCES

on Eagle Beach and the northern end of Manchebo Beach, the island's finest stretches of sand.

Taking a sailing trip

(F) Whether you go on a booze cruise or a more sedate catamaran sailing trip, one of the best things you can do in Aruba is to be out on the water. Some of these cruises take in the island's best snorkeling spots, some the beautiful views of Oranjestad twinkling in the distance at dusk. Others offer more of a party atmosphere. Whichever you choose, be prepared to be dazzled with the brilliant blues.

Splashing out at one of Aruba's big high-rise resorts

(G) Glitzy high-rise hotels line beautiful Palm Beach. Most of these come complete with a hopping casino, myriad activity options right on site, and good restaurants

for dining. But since all-inclusives are still not the norm in Aruba, you don't have to feel guilty for going into town to have dinner, though the lack of AI options also means that the restaurants at most resorts are surprisingly good.

Hiking with Aruba Nature Sensitive Hikers

(H) Eddy Croes, a former park ranger, is the owner of this outfitter that offers only small-group hikes and activities. He and his team will take you to parts of Aruba you are not likely to visit on your own. Eddy helped establish Arikok National Park and served as head ranger there, so you can be assured he knows the ins and outs of his home turf.

Trying your luck at one of the island's casinos

(I) Aruba has the best casinos in the Caribbean. In fact, this is the only island that offers anything close to the Las Vegas–style experience. Some of the better ones are the casual, independent Alhambra casino; the modern, pulsating Copacabana Casino at the Hyatt Regency Aruba; the glittering Crystal Casino at the Renaissance Aruba in Oranjestad; and the 24-hour Stellaris Casino at the Aruba Marriott.

Teeing off in paradise

(J) Constant trade winds make golf on Aruba a more challenging proposition than on many Caribbean islands. Although the landscape is arid, the stunning Tierra del Sol golf course on the island's northwest point has lush greens as well as cacti and rock formations. It's easily the island's best course.

Shopping

(K) Though Aruba is not a duty-free port, you can still find some excellent buys at the island's many shops and boutiques, whether you are looking for genuine Dutch cheeses (which are quite a good buy), hand-embroidered linens, local products made from aloe vera, or luxury watches. You can also buy Cuban cigars here, but you can't bring them back to the U.S. legally, so smoke them while you've got them.

WHEN TO GO

Aruba's high season is traditionally winter—from early December through mid-April—when northern weather is at its worst. During this season you're guaranteed the most entertainment at resorts and the most people with whom to enjoy it. It's also the most fashionable, the most expensive, and the most popular time to visit, both for people staying a week or more and for cruise-ship passengers coming ashore for just the day (and probably the night, when cruisers pack the bars along with everyone staying on the island). But the island's continuing popularity means that hotels during this period are solidly booked, and you must make reservations at least two or three months in advance for the very best places (and to get the best airfares). During the rest of the year rate reductions can be dramatic, as hotel prices drop 20% to 40% after April 15.

Climate

Aruba doesn't really have a rainy season and rarely sees a hurricane—one reason why the island is more popular than most during the off-season from mid-May through mid-November, when the risk of Atlantic hurricanes is at its highest. You certainly take fewer chances by coming here during the late summer and fall, and temperatures are constant (along with the trade winds) year-round. Expect daytime temperatures in the 80s F and nighttime temperatures in the high 70s F year-round.

Annual Events

February or March witnesses a spectacular **Carnival**, a riot of color whirling to the tunes of steel bands and culminating in the Grand Parade, where some of the floats rival the extravagance of those in the Big Easy's Mardi Gras.

Aruba's **Jazz and Latin Music Festival** is held each June, when for a few nights you can hear jazz and Latin music performed at the outdoor venue next to the Renaissance Aruba Beach Resort at Renaissance Mall.

The **Hi-Winds Pro Am Windsurfing Competition** brings windsurfers of all skill levels from more than 30 different countries during June or July to compete off the beaches at Fisherman's Huts at Hadikurari.

The **Aruba Music Festival**, a two-day event held in September or October, features international pop stars. (Sure, the artists may not have current hits, but the festival can be a fun nostalgic experience.) Past performers include Peter Frampton; REO Speedwagon, Gloria Estefan, and Pat Benatar.

GREAT ITINERARIES

Are you perplexed about which of Aruba's many beaches is best or about how to spend your time during one of the island's rare rainy days? Below are some suggestions to guide you. There are also a few ideas on how to spend a night (or two) celebrating all the perfect days you've been having.

A Perfect Day at the Beach

If you didn't bring your own, borrow or rent snorkel gear at your hotel so that you can fully appreciate the calm water and all its inhabitants. Eagle Beach is one of the island's best, and you can grab a space under one of the many palapa umbrellas if you arrive early enough. The water here is fine for both swimming and snorkeling. Be sure take in liquids regularly to avoid dehydration—rum punch may sound good, but water is probably best. As the sun goes down, hop back across the road to the very casual Pata Pata Bar at La Cabana Resort for happy hour. There's no need to change.

A Perfect Rainy Day

Even though Aruba is outside the hurricane belt, you may find yourself with a rainy day. Start off with breakfast at DeliFrance in the Certified Mega Mall, then head to downtown Oranjestad and visit some museums, perhaps the Archaeological Museum of Aruba or the Numismatic Museum. Then why wait until dinner to have an elegant meal when you can have one for lunch? Make a reservation at Le Dôme, one of Aruba's best restaurants. After lunch, head to the Mandara Spa at the Marriott Aruba Ocean Club; your body will thank you. Your soul will, too. Or if you want more activity, try the Eagle Bowling Palace. You could also take in a movie at Seaport Cinema in the Seaport Village Market Place.

A Perfect Night of Romance

Aruba is one of the most romantic places on earth, and one of the most romantic things you can do is to take a quiet sunset cruise. Try a voyage on the 43-foot sailing yacht *Tranquilo*, which includes drinks. If you don't have your sea legs yet, a sunset catamaran cruise might be more your style. Then have a romantic dinner. Pinchos Grill & Bar is hard to beat, even on an island filled with romantic dining options. After dinner, stop for a quiet drink, and end the evening with a walk—hand in hand—along the waterfront.

SNAPSHOT OF ARUBA

The Island

Aruba's topography is unusual for a Caribbean island. The southern and western coasts consist of miles of palm-lined, white-sand beaches. The calm, blue-green waters are so clear that in some areas visibility extends to a depth of 100 feet. The northeast coast is wild and rugged; here the waves pound against the coral cliffs, creating remarkable rock formations. The desertlike interior is home to various types of cacti and still more extraordinary rock formations. Divi-divi trees flourish everywhere.

Poking out of the Caribbean Sea, Aruba is at latitude 12°30' north and longitude 70° west. The island lies about 32 km (20 mi) from Venezuela's northern coast, near the Península Paraguaná. Aruba is only 32 km (20 mi) long and 10 km (6 mi) across at its widest point, with a total area of 180 square km (70 square mi).

In the east, Arikok National Park makes up 18% of the island's total area. Here you can visit 617-foot Mount Yamanota, Aruba's highest peak. The island's capital, Oranjestad, is on the southwest coast, and Dutch and Spanish influences are evident in the colorful houses along Wilhelminastraat.

Two main thoroughfares—J.E. Irausquin and L.G. Smith boulevards—link the capital to the hotels along Eagle and Palm beaches.

To the southeast lies San Nicolas, the island's second-largest metropolis and the site of an oil refinery. At Aruba's northwestern tip are large rolling sand dunes. Nestled at the island's heart, Santa Cruz is the cradle of religious culture, symbolized by a large cross marking the spot where Spanish missionaries introduced Christianity.

The People

Archaeological and genetic research indicates that the first inhabitants of Aruba, the Caquetio people, migrated to the island as early as 2500 BC. These hunter-gatherers, who most likely arrived from the nearby Venezuelan coast, had no knowledge of agriculture or pottery making. They seem to have settled in Aruba until about AD 1000, when another group of Caquetio people (often misspelled as Caiquetio) arrived from northwest Venezuela. This group brought with them pottery-making skills (this time is usually referred to as the Ceramic Period) and some agricultural knowledge. They spoke an Arawakan language (also called Caquetio), and DNA evidence suggests that they were closely related to Aruba's original tribal occupants. Signs of these early people can be found all over Aruba, including at the Tanki Flip archaeo-

logical site, and pottery and burial evidence suggests that they had a rich and well-developed culture. This ended abruptly and sadly with the arrival of the Europeans.

The date when the first Europeans set foot on Aruba is unclear. Around 1499, Spanish explorer Alonso de Ojeda (a lieutenant under Christopher Columbus) explored nearby Bonaire and Curaçao, but did not mention a third island. A map created in 1502 omits Aruba, but clearly illustrates its neighbors. Aruba was first mentioned in 1505. According to oral history, an Arawak chieftain guided the first Spanish explorers inland, where they erected a cross to mark the occasion. (In 1968 this event was commemorated by the placement of a large wooden cross atop a rocky hill in Santa Cruz.) The Spanish settlers made some efforts to bring Christianity to the local population, and even brought in a Christian cacique (native chief) from the mainland to assist them in their efforts.

Due to their lack of gold or other useful resources, the Spanish referred to Aruba, Bonaire, and Curaçao as "Islas Inutiles" or "useless islands." In 1513 the Spanish exported most of Aruba's native population to nearby Hispaniola (today's Dominican Republic and Haiti) to work in sil-

ver mines there. Some of the native people were brought back to the island in 1527, and others escaped to the mainland.

In 1636, during the Eighty Years' War between Holland and Spain, the Dutch took control of Aruba, Bonaire, and Curaçao, ruling them under the charter of the Dutch West India Company. Over the next 100 years commerce grew on the island, which served as a satellite to the administrative center on larger Curaçao.

Owing to the arid climate and poor soil, Aruba was spared from plantation economics and the slave trade; instead, the Dutch used the remaining Caquetio people to herd cattle. The Dutch held power until 1805, when the English laid claim to Aruba briefly during the Napoleonic Wars. The Dutch Republic on the European continent fell to the French in 1795, and France annexed the Netherlands in 1810. But after Napoléon's defeat in 1815 political lines throughout Europe were redrawn. The Kingdom of the Netherlands was born, and in 1816 possession of Aruba was returned permanently to the Dutch.

In 1750 Domingo Antonio Silvestre—a Venezuelan who had been converted to Catholicism by Spanish missionaries—built a small chapel at Alto Vista on the island's north shore to accommodate the

Catholic community, which until this time had had no formal place of worship. The winding approach road is lined with 12 white crosses indicating the stations of the cross, which pilgrims can follow to the tranquil chapel. The church of Santa Ana, built in the district of Noord in 1776, is renowned for its handsomely carved oak altar, which was awarded a prize for neo-Gothic design at the Rome exhibition of 1870. Interestingly, the original 200-year-old Spanish cross from the Alto Vista chapel now resides here as well.

The first Protestant church was built in 1848 in the center of Oranjestad. Today the original building houses a museum that is maintained by the congregation; an adjoining larger church is used for weekly services. Another landmark house of worship, the Immaculada Concepción church in Santa Cruz, is noted for the colorful biblical mural decorating its nave. The Beth Israel synagogue was built in 1962 to meet the needs of the growing Jewish community. (A congregation began forming as early as the 1920s, when an international workforce was drawn to Aruba to staff the oil refinery.)

With a history full of cultures clashing and melding, it's no surprise that most islanders are fluent in several languages. School lessons are taught in Dutch, the official language. Arubans begin studying English, recognized as the international tongue, in the fourth grade. Spanish, essential because of Aruba's proximity to South America, is taught in school as early as the fifth grade, and French is offered as an option in high school. In normal conversation, however, the locals speak Papiamento—a mix of Spanish, Dutch, Portuguese, English, and French, as well as Indian and African languages. Since 1998 Papiamento has also been taught in grade school.

The Economy

Due to its dry climate and poor soil, Aruba was basically unused by the colonists until the Dutch introduced horses and cattle. They enlisted the locals to be herders, and Aruba was a convenient livestock and meat depot for many years. As more colonists arrived from Curaçao and Brazil in the 1700s, the economy began a lazy evolution. Then in the 19th century Aruba's cycle of boom and bust began with the discovery of gold in Rooi Fluit in 1824. The ensuing rush helped breathe new life into the sleepy island.

The gold industry exploded and the population swelled as immigrants flowed in from neighboring islands and the mainland. Aruba soon became an important sup-

plier of gold, and by 1916—when supplies were depleted—close to 3 million pounds of gold had been extracted. The remnants of the gold industry can still be seen at the gold-smelter ruins in Bushiri. During the time of the gold rush, the island also became a major supplier of aloe vera, divi-divi pods (used for tanning leather), and calcium phosphate. These industries, however, were not able to support the economy after the gold industry closed, and the island fell into another slump.

Aruba ended this economic downturn by opening an oil refinery. Though the island has no oil resources of its own, it's well positioned to be a processing and shipment point for oil from Venezuela. In 1926 workers began blasting away the reef on the southern coast near San Nicholas, and the harbor was dredged to allow large ships to enter. Then in 1928 the Royal Dutch Shell Company opened the Eagle Oil Refinery. Oil was shipped into Aruba from Lake Maracaibo in Venezuela by the Lago Transportation Company of Canada (which eventually opened its own refinery on the island). By 1929 the new refinery was producing more than 200,000 barrels a day. Huge numbers of migrant workers arrived to satisfy the demands for labor, which helped fuel a population boom and added to an increas-

ingly cosmopolitan society. At its height, the oil industry employed more than 8,000 workers—about 16% of the island's population.

The importance of Aruba's oil refining was made obvious during World War II. Aruba, Curaçao, and the nearby British island of Trinidad were key Allied supply depots in the Caribbean, and German U-boats were sent to close them down. In 1942 the harbor and the Lago refinery at San Nicholas were bombed. Two tankers were hit by torpedoes, but an accident aboard the German U-156 disabled its deck guns, and the refinery was spared. There is no doubt that Hitler, at the time, viewed the destruction of Aruba's oil production as a key strategy for winning the war. The oil industry continued to grow despite the threats of attack, reaching a peak production of 550,000 barrels a day in 1965.

Because of an unstable oil market, the refinery was closed in 1985. The Coastal Corporation of Texas reopened it in 1991 (and it now produces 150,000 barrels a day), but the tourist trade has replaced oil as Aruba's primary source of income. Education, health care, and other public services are financed by tourism, which has also helped to keep the unemployment rate at less than 1%. Because of this, it's no surprise that guests

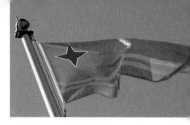

are warmly received. This warmth has, in turn, contributed to a general upward trend in the number of visitors—from 206,750 in 1985 to more than 800,000 in 2004.

The Government

Until late 1985 Aruba was a member of the Netherlands Antilles, along with Bonaire, Curaçao, St. Maarten, St. Eustatius, and Saba. On January 1, 1986, Aruba was granted a new status as an independent entity within the Kingdom of the Netherlands, which now consists of the Netherlands, the Netherlands Antilles, and Aruba.

The island has a royally appointed governor, who acts as the Dutch sovereign's representative for a six-year term. Executive power is held by the seven-member council of ministers, appointed by the legislative council for four-year terms and presided over by the prime minister, who is elected every four years. The legislature consists of a parliament whose 21 members are elected by popular vote to serve four-year terms. Legal jurisdiction lies with the Common Court of Justice of Aruba and the Netherlands Antilles as well as the Supreme Court of Justice at The Hague in the Netherlands. Defense and foreign affairs still fall under the realm of the kingdom, whereas internal matters involving such things as customs, immigration, aviation, and communications are handled autonomously.

The Language

Papiamento is hybrid language born out of the colorful past of Aruba, Bonaire, and Curaçao. The language's use is generally thought to have started in the 17th century when Sephardic Jews migrated with their African slaves from Brazil to Curaçao. The slaves spoke a pidgin Portuguese, which may have been blended with pure Portuguese, some Dutch (the colonial power in charge of the island), and Arawakan. Proximity to the mainland meant that Spanish and English words were also incorporated.

Papiamento is roughly translated as "the way of speaking." (Sometimes the suffix -*mentu* is spelled in the Spanish and Portuguese way [-*mento*], creating the variant spelling.) It began as an oral tradition, handed down through the generations and spoken by all social classes on the islands. There's no uniform spelling or grammar from island to island, or even from one neighborhood to another. However, it is also beginning to receive some official recognition. A noteworthy measure of the increased government respect for the language is that anyone applying for citizenship must be fluent in both Papiamento and Dutch.

Exploring

WORD OF MOUTH

"Aruba is a lot of fun to drive around . . . outside of Oranjestad, the road maps only sort of approximate the real roads, but since it's a small and very friendly island, it's no problem!"

—dlundgren

BALMY SUNSHINE, SILKY SAND, AQUAMARINE WATERS, natural scenic wonders, outstanding dining, decent shopping, and an array of nightly entertainment . . . Aruba's got it in spades. It's also unusual in its range of choices, from world-class oceanfront resorts equipped with gourmet restaurants and high-dollar casinos to intimate neighborhood motels and diners not far off the beach.

Aruba's wildly sculpted landscape is replete with rocky deserts, cactus clusters, secluded coves, blue vistas, and the trademark divi-divi tree. To preserve the environment while encouraging visitors to explore, the government has implemented an ongoing ecotourism plan. Initiatives include finding ways to make efficient use of the limited land resources and protecting the natural and cultural resources in such preserves as Arikok National Park and the Coastal Protection Zone (along the island's north and east coasts).

Oranjestad, Aruba's capital, is good for shopping by day and dining by night, but the "real Aruba"—with its untamed beauty—can be found only in the countryside. Rent a car, take a sightseeing tour, or hire a cab by the hour to explore. Though desolate, the northern and eastern shores are striking and well worth a visit. A drive out past the California Lighthouse or to Seroe Colorado will give you a feel for the backcountry.

Although the main highways are well paved, the windward side of the island still has some roads that are a mixture of compacted dirt and stones. A car is fine, but a four-wheel-drive vehicle will enable you to better navigate the unpaved interior. Remember that few beaches outside the hotel strip along Palm and Eagle beaches to the west have refreshment stands, so pack your own food and drink. Aside from those in the infrequent restaurant, there are no public bathrooms outside of Oranjestad.

Traffic is sparse, but signs leading to sights are often small and hand-lettered (this is slowly changing as the government puts up official road signs), so watch closely. Route 1A travels southbound along the western coast, and 1B is simply northbound along the same road. If you lose your way, just follow the divi-divi trees.

Numbers in the margin correspond to points of interest in the text and on the Exploring map.

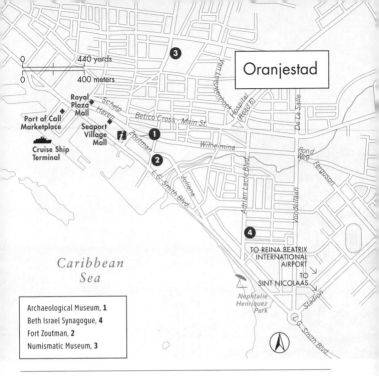

Archaeological Museum, **1**
Beth Israel Synagogue, **4**
Fort Zoutman, **2**
Numismatic Museum, **3**

ORANJESTAD

Aruba's charming capital is best explored on foot. Its palm-lined central thoroughfare runs between old and new pastel-painted buildings of typical Dutch design (Spanish influence is also evident in some of the architecture). There are many malls with boutiques and shops; downtown and Seaport Village are the major shopping areas. Every morning the wharf teems with activity as merchants sell produce and fresh fish—often right off their boats. You can also buy handicrafts and T-shirts at this dockside bazaar, where bargaining is expected and dollars or florins are accepted. Island schooners and houseboats anchored near the fishing boats add to the port's ambience. Wilhelmina Park, a small tropical garden on the waterfront along L.G. Smith Boulevard, has a sculpture of the Netherlands' Queen Wilhelmina, who reigned from 1890 to 1948.

TIMING

There is rarely a day when at least two cruise ships aren't docked in Oranjestad, so the downtown shopping area is usually bustling. Some of the smaller stores are closed on

DID YOU KNOW?

Aruba's first Dutch colonial governor was Peter Stuyvesant, who was also the last Dutch Director-General of New Amsterdam, which is perhaps better known today as New York.

Sunday, but virtually all the larger ones are open to accommodate cruise passengers looking for bargains. When there are more than two ships in port, expect lines at retail outlets and long waits at restaurants.

WHAT TO SEE

❶ **Archaeological Museum of Aruba.** Aruba's small museum has two rooms chock-full of fascinating artifacts from the indigenous Arawak people, including farm and domestic utensils dating back hundreds of years. ⊠*J. E. Irausquin Blvd. 2A* ☎*297/582–8979* ⊡*Free* ⊙*Weekdays 8–noon and 1–4.*

❹ **Beth Israel Synagogue.** Built in 1962, this synagogue is the only Jewish house of worship on Aruba, and it strives to meet the needs of its Ashkenazi, Sephardic, European, North American, and South American worshippers. The island's Jewish community dates back to the opening of the oil refinery in the 1920s, when small congregations gathered in private homes in San Nicolas. The temple holds regular services on Friday at 8 PM and on Saturday at 8 AM; additional services are held on high holy days. Visitors are always welcome, although it's best to make an appointment to see the synagogue when there's not a service. A Judaica shop sells keepsakes, kosher dry goods, and kiddush wines. ⊠*Adrian Laclé Blvd. 2* ☎*297/582–3272* ⊡*Free except high holy days.*

❷ **Fort Zoutman.** One of the island's oldest edifices, Aruba's historic fort was built in 1796 and played an important role in skirmishes between British and Curaçao troops in 1803. The Willem III Tower, named for the Dutch monarch of that time, was added in 1868 to serve as a lighthouse. Over time the fort has been a government office building, a police station, and a prison; now its historical museum displays Aruban artifacts in an 18th-century house. ⊠*Zoutmanstraat* ☎*297/582–6099* ⊡*Free* ⊙*Weekdays 8–noon and 1–4.*

❸ **Numismatic Museum.** This museum displays more than 40,000 historic coins and paper money from around the world. A few pieces were salvaged from shipwrecks in the region. Some of the coins circulated during the Roman Empire, the Byzantine Empire, and the ancient Chinese dynasties; the oldest dates from the 3rd century BC. The museum had its start as the private collection of an Aruban who dug up some old coins in his garden. It's now run by his grand-

Papiamento Primer

CLOSE UP

Arubans enjoy it when visitors use their language, so don't be shy. You can buy a Papiamento dictionary to build your vocabulary, but here are a few pleasantries—including some terms of friendship and love— to get you started:

Bon dia. Good morning.

Bon tardi. Good afternoon.

Bon nochi. Good evening/ night.

Bon bini. Welcome.

Ajo. Bye.

Te aworo. See you later.

Pasa un bon dia. Have a good day.

Danki. Thank you.

Na bo ordo. You're welcome.

Con ta bai? How are you?

Mi ta bon. I am fine.

Ban goza! Let's enjoy!

Pabien! Congratulations!

Quanto costa esaki? How much is this?

Hopi bon Very good

Ami Me

Abo You

Nos dos The two of us

Mi dushi My sweetheart

Ku tur mi amor With all my love

Un braza A hug

Un sunchi A kiss

Ranka lenga To French kiss

Mi stima Aruba I love Aruba.

---

daughter. ⊠ *Weststraat, Oranjestad* ☎*297/582–8831* ⚏*$5* ⊗*Mon.–Thurs. 9–4, Fri. 9–1, Sat. 9–noon.*

WESTERN ARUBA

Western Aruba is where you'll likely spend most of your time. All the resorts and time-shares are along this coast, most of them clustered on the oceanfront strip at the luscious Palm and Eagle beaches, in the city of Oranjestad, or in the district of Noord. All the casinos, major shopping malls, and most restaurants are found in this region, as is the airport.

A GOOD TOUR

Rent a car and head out on Route 1A toward **Oranjestad** for some sightseeing and shopping. Pick up Route 1B out of town. At a large roundabout turn right and drive for about 1 km (½ mi), then make another right at the first intersection and drive for ½ km (¼ mi) until you reach the fields and factory of **Aruba Aloe**. Head back to the roundabout and pick up Route 4A. Follow this road a short way to the **Ayo and Casibari Rock Formations**. Continue on 4A and

Aruba

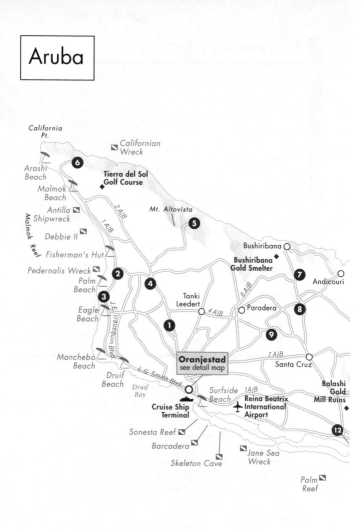

California Pt.

Californian Wreck

Arashi Beach

6

Tierra del Sol Golf Course

Malmok Beach

Antilla Shipwreck

Debbie II

2 A/B

1 A/B

Mt. Altovista

5

Malmok Reef

Fisherman's Hut

Pedernalis Wreck

2

Palm Beach

3

4

Tanki Leedert

4 A/B

Bushiribana

Bushiribana Gold Smelter

7

Andicouri

Paradera

8

J.E. Irausquin Blvd.

Eagle Beach

1

6 A/B

9

Manchebo Beach

Druif Beach

Druif Bay

L.G. Smith Blvd.

7 A/B

Santa Cruz

Balashi Gold Mill Ruins

Oranjestad
see detail map

Surfside Beach

1 A/B

Reina Beatrix International Airport

12

Cruise Ship Terminal

Sonesta Reef

Barcadera

Skeleton Cave

Jane Sea Wreck

Palm Reef

0   4 mi
0   6 km

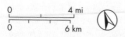

Alto Vista Chapel, **5**

Arikok National Park, **10**

Aruba Aloe, **1**

Aruba Ostrich Farm, **7**

Balashi Brewery, **12**

Bubali Bird Sanctuary, **3**

Butterfly Farm, **2**

California Lighthouse, **6**

Frenchman's Pass, **11**

Mt. Hooiberg, **9**

Noord, **4**

Rock Formations, **8**

San Nicolas, **14**

Savaneta, **13**

Seroe Colorado, **15**

C a r i b b e a n   S e a

10

ARIKOK NATIONAL PARK

Mt. Arikok

○ *Miralamar*

🏖 *Dos Playa*

🏖 *Boca Prins (sand dunes)*

Fontein Cave

Guadikin Cave

Baranca Sunu

11

Spanish Lagoon

Masiduri Cave

Mt. Yamanota

1 A/B

1 B

Boca Grandi

🏖 *Bachelor's Beach*

1 A

13

Mangel Halto (Savaneta)

◩ *Mangel Halto Reef (Pos Chiquito Reef)*

Santa Largo Beach

🏖 *Grapefield Beach*

1 A

14

🏖 *Coco's Beach*

◩ *Isla di Oro*

Baby Beach

15

Natural Bridge

Colorado Pt.

◩ *Captain Wreck*

◩ *Shark Caves*

KEY	
🏖	*Beaches*
◩	*Dive Sites*

follow the signs for **Hooiberg**; if you're so inclined, climb the steps of Haystack Hill. Return on 4B to 6A and drive a couple of miles to the Bushiribana Gold Smelter. Beyond it on the windward coast is the **Aruba Ostrich Farm**.

From here take 6B to the intersection of Route 3B, which you'll follow into the town of **Noord**, a good place to stop for lunch. Then take Route 2B, following the signs for the branch road leading to the **Alto Vista Chapel**. Return to town and pick up 2B and then 1B to reach the **California Lighthouse**. In this area you can also see Arashi Beach (a popular snorkeling site) and the Tierra del Sol golf course. From the lighthouse follow 1A back toward Palm Beach. On the way, stop at the **Butterfly Farm** and the **Bubali Bird Sanctuary**.

TIMING

If you head out right after breakfast, you can just about complete the tour above in one very full day. If you want to linger in Oranjestad's shops or go snorkeling along the beach, consider breaking the tour up into two days.

WHAT TO SEE

❺ Alto Vista Chapel. Alone near the island's northwest corner sits the scenic little Alto Vista Chapel. The wind whistles through the simple mustard-color walls, eerie boulders, and looming cacti. Along the side of the road back to civilization are miniature crosses with depictions of the stations of the cross and hand-lettered signs exhorting PRAY FOR US, SINNERS and the like—a simple yet powerful evocation of faith. To get here, follow the rough, winding dirt road that loops around the island's northern tip, or from the hotel strip take Palm Beach Road through three intersections and watch for the asphalt road to the left just past the Alto Vista Rum Shop.

❶ Aruba Aloe. Learn all about aloe—its cultivation, processing, and production—at Aruba's own aloe farm and factory. Guided tours lasting about a half hour will show you how the gel—revered for its skin-soothing properties—is extracted from the aloe vera plant and used in a variety of products, including after-sun creams, soaps, and shampoos. Though not the most exciting tour on the island—and unlikely to keeps kids entertained—it might be a good option in the event of a rainy day. You can purchase the finished goods in the gift shop. ⊠*Pitastraat 115* ☎*297/588–3222* ☞*$8* ☉ *Weekdays 8:30–4:30, Sat. 9–1.*

Alto Vista Chapel, on the windy northwest coast of Aruba, was built in 1750.

7 ★ **Aruba Ostrich Farm.** Everything you ever wanted to know about the world's largest living birds can be found at this farm. A large palapa houses a gift shop and restaurant (popular with large bus tours), and tours of the farm are available every half hour. This operation is virtually identical to the facility in Curaçao; it's owned by the same company. ⊠*Makividiri Rd., Paradera* ☎*297/585–9630* ⊕*www.arubaostrichfarm.com* ⊴*$12* ⊙*Daily 9–5.*

12 **Balashi Brewery.** The factory that manufactures the excellent local beer, Balashi, offers daily tours to the public that will take you through every stage of the brewing process. It makes for a fascinating hour, and the price of the tour includes a free drink at the end. Those more interested in beer drinking than beer making might want to visit the factory any evening from 7 to 10 for happy hour (there is live music on Friday). ⊠*Balashi 75, Balashi* ☎*297/592–2544* ⊕*www.balashi.com.*

3 **Bubali Bird Sanctuary.** Bird-watchers delight in the more than 80 species of migratory birds that nest in this wetlands area inland from the island's strip of high-rise hotels. Herons, egrets, cormorants, coots, gulls, skimmers, terns, and ducks are among the winged wonders in and around the two interconnected artificial lakes that make up the sanctuary. ⊠*J. E. Irausquin Blvd., Noord* ☎*No phone* ⊴*Free.*

DID YOU KNOW?

Unlike the idyllic beaches of the south and west, Aruba's northeast coast, which faces the open Caribbean, is pounded by fierce waves pushed inland from near-constant trade winds.

The Divi-Divi Tree

Like a statuesque dancer in a graceful flat-back pose, the *watapana*, or divi-divi tree, is one of Aruba's hallmarks. Oddly enough, this tropical shrub is a member of the legume family. Its astringent pods contain high levels of tannin, which is leached out for tanning leather. The pods also yield a black dye. The tree has a moderate rate of growth and a high drought tolerance. Typically it reaches no more than 25 feet in height, with a flattened crown and irregular, forked branches. Its leaves are dull green, and its inconspicuous yet fragrant flowers are pale yellow or white and grow in small clusters. Thanks to constant trade winds, the divi-divis serve as a natural compass: they're bent toward the island's leeward—or western—side, where most of the hotels are.

❷ **Butterfly Farm.** Hundreds of butterflies from around the world flutter about this spectacular garden. Guided 20- to 30-minute tours (included in the price of admission) provide an entertaining look into the life cycle of these insects, from egg to caterpillar to chrysalis to butterfly. There's a special deal offered here: after your initial visit, you can return as often as you like for free during your vacation. ✉ *J. E. Irausquin Blvd., Palm Beach* ☎ *297/586–3656* ⊕ *www.the butterflyfarm.com* ⍐ *$13* ⊙ *Daily 9–4:30; last tour at 4.*

❻ **California Lighthouse.** The lighthouse, built by a French architect in 1910, stands at the island's far northern end. Although you can't go inside, you can ascend the hill to the lighthouse base for some great views. In this stark landscape you might feel as though you've just landed on the moon. The lighthouse is surrounded by huge boulders that look like extraterrestrial monsters and sand dunes embroidered with scrub that resembles undulating sea serpents.

❾ **Mount Hooiberg.** Named for its shape (*hooiberg* means "haystack" in Dutch), this 541-foot peak lies inland just past the airport. If you have the energy, climb the 562 steps to the top for an impressive view of Oranjestad (and Venezuela on clear days).

❹ **Noord.** The district of Noord is home to the strip of high-rise hotels and casinos that line Palm Beach. Here you can also find the beautiful **St. Ann's Church,** known for its ornate 19th-century altar. In this area Aruban-style homes are scattered amid clusters of cacti.

Aruba's divi-divi trees are always bent toward the west, where you'll find the best beaches.

⑧ Rock Formations. The massive boulders at Ayo and Casibari are a mystery, as they don't match the island's geological makeup. You can climb to the top for fine views of the arid countryside. On the way you'll doubtless pass Aruba whiptail lizards—the males are cobalt blue, and the females are blue-gray with light-blue dots. The main path to Casibari has steps and handrails the entire way (except on one side), and you must move through tunnels and along narrow steps and ledges to reach the top. At Ayo you can find ancient pictographs in a small cave (the entrance has iron bars to protect the drawings from vandalism). You may also encounter boulder climbers, who are increasingly drawn to Ayo's smooth surfaces. Access to Casibari is via Tanki Highway 4A; you can reach Ayo via Route 6A. Watch carefully for the turnoff signs near the center of the island on the way to the windward side.

EASTERN ARUBA

In addition to the vast Arikok National Park, eastern Aruba is home to the island's second-largest city, San Nicolas, and several charming fishing villages and pristine beaches. Here you can get a real sense of traditional island life.

DID YOU KNOW?

As many as 80 different bird species can be spotted at Bubali Bird Sanctuary, which consists of wetlands fed by purified water from the island's sewage-treatment plant.

CLOSE UP

Cunucu Houses

Pastel houses surrounded by cacti fences adorn Aruba's flat, rugged *cunucu* ("country" in Papiamento). The features of these traditional houses were developed in response to the environment. Early settlers discovered that slanting roofs allowed the heat to rise and that small windows helped to keep in the cool air. Among the earliest building materials was *caliche*, a durable calcium-carbonate substance found in the island's southeastern hills. Many houses were also built using interlocking coral rocks that didn't require mortar (this technique is no longer used, thanks to cement and concrete). Contemporary design combines some of the basic principles of the earlier homes with touches of modernization: windows, though still narrow, have been elongated; roofs are constructed of bright tiles; pretty patios have been added; and doorways and balconies present an ornamental face to the world beyond.

A GOOD TOUR

Take Route 1A to Route 4B and visit the Balashi Gold Smelter ruins and **Frenchman's Pass**. Return to 1A and continue your drive past Mangel Halto Beach to **Savaneta**, a fishing village and one of several residential areas that have examples of typical Aruban homes. Follow 1A to **San Nicolas**, where you can meander along the main promenade, pick up a few souvenirs, and grab a bite to eat. Heading out of town, continue on 1A until you hit a fork in the road; follow the signs toward **Seroe Colorado**, with the nearby natural bridge and the Colorado Point Lighthouse. From here follow the signs toward Rodgers Beach, just one of several area shores where you can kick back for a while. Nearby Baby Beach, with calm waters and beautiful white sand, is a favorite spot for snorkelers. To the north, on Route 7B, is Boca Grandi, a great windsurfing spot. Next is Grapefield Beach, a stretch of white sand that glistens against a backdrop of cliffs and boulder formations. Shortly beyond it, on 7B, you'll come into **Arikok National Park**, where you can explore caves and tunnels, play on sand dunes, and tackle Mount Yamanota, Aruba's highest elevation. Farther along 7B is Santa Cruz, where a wooden cross stands atop a hill to mark the spot where Christianity was introduced to the islanders. The same highway will bring you all the way into Oranjestad.

TIMING

You can see most of Eastern Aruba's sights in a half-day, though it's easy to fill a full day if you spend time relaxing on a sandy beach or exploring the trails in Arikok National Park.

WHAT TO SEE

❿ Arikok National Wildlife Park. Nearly 20% of Aruba has been designated part of this national park, which sprawls across the eastern interior and the northeast coast. The park is the keystone of the government's long-term ecotourism plan to preserve Aruba's resources and showcases the island's flora and fauna as well as ancient Arawak petroglyphs, the ruins of a gold-mining operation at Miralmar, and the remnants of Dutch peasant settlements at Masiduri. At the park's main entrance, Arikok Center houses offices, restrooms, and food facilities. All visitors must stop here upon entering, so that officials can manage the traffic flow and hand out information on park rules and features. Within the confines of the park are Mount Arikok and the 620-foot Mount Yamanota, Aruba's highest peak.

Anyone looking for geological exotica should head for the park's caves, found on the northeastern coast. Baranca Sunu, the so-called Tunnel of Love, has a heart-shape entrance and naturally sculpted rocks farther inside that look like the Madonna, Abraham Lincoln, and even a jaguar. Fontein Cave, which was used by indigenous peoples centuries ago, is marked with ancient drawings (rangers are on hand to offer explanations). Bats are known to

DID YOU KNOW?

Scientists do not know the geological origins of massive Calibari Rock, but you can climb to the top and may see a blue Aruba whiptail lizard on the way.

make appearances—don't worry, they won't bother you. Although you don't need a flashlight because the paths are well lighted, it's best to wear sneakers.

⓫ **Frenchman's Pass.** Overhanging trees and towering cacti border this luscious stretch of road. The pass is almost midway between Oranjestad and San Nicolas; follow L.G. Smith Boulevard past a shimmering vista of blue-green sea and turn off where you see the drive-in theater (a popular local hangout). Then proceed to the first intersection, turn right, and follow the curve to the right. Gold was discovered on Aruba in 1824, and near Frenchman's Pass are the massive concrete-and-limestone ruins of the **Balashi Gold Smelter,** a lovely place to picnic and listen to the chattering parakeets. A magnificent, gnarled divi-divi tree guards the entrance. The area now is home to Aruba's desalination plant, where all of the island's drinking water is purified.

⓮ **San Nicolas.** During the oil-refinery heyday, Aruba's oldest village was a bustling port; now its primary purpose is tourism. *The* institution in town is Charlie's Restaurant and Bar. Stop in for a drink and advice on what to see and do in this little town. Aruba's main red-light district is located here, and will be fairly apparent to even the most casual observer.

⓭ **Savaneta.** The Dutch settled here after retaking the island in 1816, and it served as Aruba's first capital. Today it's a bustling fishing village with a 150-year-old *cas de torto* (mud hut), the oldest dwelling still standing on the island.

⓯ **Seroe Colorado.** What was originally built as a community for oil workers is known for its intriguing 1939 chapel. The site is surreal, as organ-pipe cacti form the backdrop for sedate whitewashed cottages. The real reason to come here is a **natural bridge.** Keep bearing east past the community, continuing uphill until you run out of road. You can then hike down to the cathedral-like formation. It's not too strenuous, but watch your footing as you descend. Be sure to follow the white arrows painted on the rocks, as there are no other directional signs. Although this bridge isn't as spectacular as its more celebrated sibling (which collapsed in 2005), the raw elemental power of the sea that created it, replete with hissing blowholes, certainly is.

Where to Eat

WORD OF MOUTH

" Dining is excellent. Our favorite was in town and is called El Gauchos. It is an Argentinian steakhouse. Also, we liked a place called Chalet Suisse."

—girlonthego

THERE ARE A FEW HUNDRED RESTAURANTS ON ARUBA, from elegant eateries to seafront shacks, so you're bound to find something to tantalize your taste buds. You can sample a wide range of cuisines—Italian, French, Argentine, Asian, and Cuban, to name a few—reflecting Aruba's eclectic blend of cultures. Chefs have to be creative on this tiny island, because of the limited number of locally grown ingredients: *maripampoen* (a vegetable that's often stewed with meat and potatoes), *hierba di hole* (a sweet-spicy herb used in fish soup), and *shimarucu* (a fruit similar to the cherry) are among the few.

Although most resorts offer better-than-average dining, don't be afraid to try one of the many excellent independent places. Ask locals about their favorite spots; some of the lesser-known restaurants offer food that's reasonably priced and definitely worth sampling.

Most restaurants on the western side of the island are along Palm Beach or in downtown Oranjestad, both easily accessible by taxi or bus. If you're heading to a restaurant in Oranjestad for dinner, leave about 15 minutes earlier than you think you should; in-town traffic can become ugly once beach hours are over. Some restaurants in Savaneta and San Nicolas are worth the trip; a car is the best way to get there. Breakfast lovers are in luck. For quantity, check out the buffets at the Hyatt, Marriott, or Wyndham resorts or local joints such as DeliFrance.

PRICES AND DRESS

Aruba's elegant restaurants—where you might have to dress up a little (jackets for men, sundresses for women)—can be pricey. If you want to spend fewer florins, opt for the more casual spots, where being comfortable is the only dress requirement. A sweater draped over your shoulders will go a long way against the chill of air-conditioning. If you plan to eat in the open air, bring along insect repellent in case the mosquitoes get unruly.

RESERVATIONS

To ensure that you get to eat at the restaurants of your choice, make some calls when you get to the island—especially during high season—to secure reservations. Note that on Sunday you may have a hard time finding a restaurant that's open for lunch, and that many eateries are closed for dinner on Sunday or Monday.

Best Bets for Aruba Dining

3

With the many restaurants to choose from, how will you decide where to eat? Fodor's writers and editors have selected their favorite restaurants in the Best Bets lists below. The Fodor's Choice properties represent the "best of the best." Find specific details about a restaurant in the full reviews.

Fodor's Choice: Flying Fishbone; Marandi; Pinchos Grill & Bar; Papamiento; Madame Janette's.

Best Budget Eats: Charlie's

Restaurant & Bar; Coco Plum; Cuba's Cookin'; DeliFrance.

Best for Families: Charlie's Restaurant & Bar; El Gaucho Argentine Grill; Hostaria Da' Vittorio.

Most Romantic: Flying Fishbone; Papamiento; The Pirates' Nest; Pinchos Grill & Bar; Passion's; Marandi; Ruinas Del Mar; Ventanas Del Mar.

Best for Local Aruban Cuisine: Gasparito Restaurant & Art Gallery; Old Cunucu House; Papamiento; The Pirate's Nest.

DINING PLANS

To give visitors an affordable way to sample the island's eclectic cuisine, the **Aruba Gastronomic Association** (*AGA* ✉*Rooi Santo 21, Noord* ☎*297/586–2161, 800/477–2896 in U.S.* ⊕*www.arubadining.com*) has created a Dine-Around program involving more than 20 island restaurants. Here's how it works: you can buy tickets for three dinners ($117 per person), five dinners ($190), seven dinners ($262), or five breakfasts or lunches plus four dinners ($230). Dinners include an appetizer, an entrée, dessert, coffee or tea, and a service charge (except when a restaurant is a VIP member, in which case $38 will be deducted from your final bill instead). Other programs, such as gift certificates and coupons for dinners at the association's VIP member restaurants, are also available. You can buy Dine-Around tickets using the association's online order form, through travel agents, or at the De Palm Tours sales desk in many hotels. Participating restaurants change frequently; the AGA Web site has the latest information.

TIPPING

Most restaurants add a service charge of 15%. It's not necessary to tip once a service charge is on the bill, but if the service is exceptional an additional tip of 10% is always appreciated. If no service charge is included on the final bill, then leave the customary tip of 15% to 20%.

WHAT IT COSTS IN U.S. DOLLARS				
¢	$	$$	$$$	$$$$
A MAIN COURSE AT DINNER				
under $8	$8–$12	$12–$20	$20–$30	over $30

Prices are per person for a main course at dinner, excluding service charges or taxes.

PALM BEACH

$$$$ ✕**Amazonia Churrascaria.** *Steak.* Bring a hearty appetite to this prix-fixe eatery. The emphasis is on meat, but the sweeping salad bar (separately priced) allows calorie counters to indulge as well. Bare brick walls, floral displays, and colorful paintings make for an intimate dining experience. Amazonia participates in AGA's Dine-Around program. ⊠*J.E. Irausquin Blvd. 374, Palm Beach* ☎*297/586–4444* ⊕*www. amazonia-aruba.com* ⊟*AE, DC, MC, V* ⊘*No lunch.*

$$$– ✕**Aqua Grill.** *Seafood.* Aficionados flock here to enjoy a wide
$$$$ selection of seafood and the largest raw bar on the island.
★ The atmosphere is casual, with a distinctly New England feel. Things can get a little noisy in the open dining room, especially when kids are underfoot (which is often), but a few sips of wine from the extensive list should help numb the effect. Maine lobster and Alaskan king crab legs are available, but why try the usual fare when you can order the Fisherman's Pot, which is filled with everything from scallops to monkfish? The wood grill serves up great low-cal

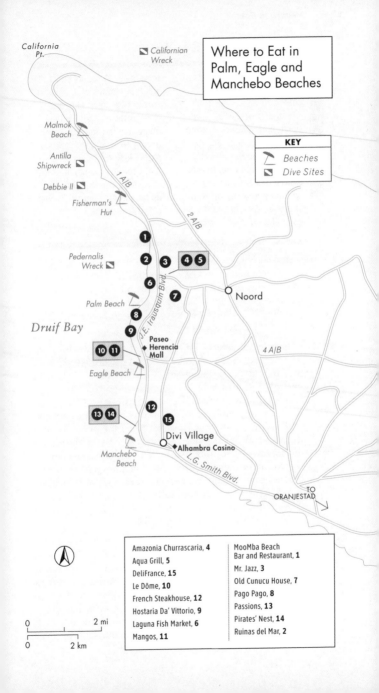

California Pt.

☒ Californian Wreck

Where to Eat in Palm, Eagle and Manchebo Beaches

Malmok Beach

Antilla Shipwreck ☒

Debbie II ☒

Fisherman's Hut

1 A/B

2 A/B

KEY

☇ Beaches
☒ Dive Sites

Pedernalis Wreck ☒

① ② ③ ④ ⑤

⑥ ⑦

Noord

Palm Beach

⑧

⑨

Druif Bay

⑩ ⑪

♦ Paseo Herencia Mall

Eagle Beach

4 A/B

⑬ ⑭

⑫

⑮

Divi Village

♦ Alhambra Casino

Manchebo Beach

L.G. Smith Blvd.

TO ORANJESTAD

J.E. Irausquin Blvd.

0 ——— 2 mi

0 ——— 2 km

Amazonia Churrascaria, **4**	MooMba Beach Bar and Restaurant, **1**
Aqua Grill, **5**	Mr. Jazz, **3**
DeliFrance, **15**	Old Cunucu House, **7**
Le Dôme, **10**	Pago Pago, **8**
French Steakhouse, **12**	Passions, **13**
Hostaria Da' Vittorio, **9**	Pirates' Nest, **14**
Laguna Fish Market, **6**	Ruinas del Mar, **2**
Mangos, **11**	

The Goods on Gouda

Each year Holland exports more than 250,000 tons of cheese to more than 100 countries, and Gouda (the Dutch pronounce it *how*-da) is one of the most popular. Gouda, named for the city where it's produced, travels well and gets harder, saltier, and more flavorful as it ages. There are six types of Gouda: young (at least 4 weeks old), semi-major (8 weeks old), major (4 months old), ultr-amajor (7 months old), old (10 months old), and vintage (more than a year old). When buying cheese in shops in Aruba, look for the control seal that confirms the name of the cheese, its country of origin, its fat content, and that it was officially inspected.

treats, such as mahimahi. There are restaurants that serve better-prepared seafood meals on the island, but the variety of offerings here is above and beyond. The restaurant is an AGA VIP member. ⊠*J. E. Irausquin Blvd. 374, Palm Beach* ☎*297/586–5900* ⊕*www.aqua-grill.com* ⊟*AE, D, MC, V* ⊗*No lunch.*

$$–$$$ ✕**Hostaria Da' Vittorio.** *Italian.* Part of the fun at this family-oriented spot is watching chef Vittorio Muscariello prepare authentic Italian regional specialties in the open kitchen. The staff helps you choose wines from the extensive list and recommends portions of hot and cold antipasti, risottos, and pastas. Those on a tight budget should stick to the pizzas; main courses bring the prices up into the higher registers. Sadly, service can be a bit dismissive during busy periods. Be aware that the decibel level of the crowd can be high. As you leave, pick up some limoncello (the famed lemon liqueur) or olive oil at the gourmet shop. A 15% gratuity is automatically added to your bill. It's an AGA VIP member. ⊠*L. G. Smith Blvd. 380, Palm Beach* ☎*297/586–3838* ⊟*AE, D, MC, V.*

$$$– ✕**Laguna.** *Caribbean.* Louvered plantation-style doors frame
$$$$ the view at this colorful restaurant. You can dine inside in air-cooled comfort or outside on the terrace overlooking the lagoon. From Monday through Saturday a different themed buffet is on offer each night with an emphasis on seafood. While the quality of the buffet food is unlikely to win any culinary awards, it is popular with the pile-high crowd. Those valuing quality over quantity may opt to

order from the à la carte menu. The service can be a bit erratic during dinner, but the breakfast buffet is good and reasonably priced. ⊠*Radisson Aruba Resort & Casino, J. E. Irausquin Blvd. 81, Palm Beach* ☎297/586–6555 ⊕*www. lagunaaruba.com* ⊟*AE, D, DC, MC, V* ⊘*No lunch.*

$$–$$$ ✕**MooMba Beach Bar & Restaurant.** *American.* Drop by anytime—this festive eatery serves breakfast, lunch, and dinner, and the menu includes a wide selection of seafood and meat specialties. It is probably best to stick with the grilled seafood courses, as the quality of other items can be erratic and especially so during busy periods. By day, sit beneath the giant palapa if you want to beat the heat, or plant yourself at a table in the sand if you haven't had enough sun. Come straight from the beach—bare feet are expected here. MooMba is popular with locals, so you can learn a bit about Aruban culture over sunset cocktails. Once a month the place is rollicking after hours with a full-moon dance party that lures all the island's night owls. It's on Palm Beach between the Marriott Surf Club and the Holiday Inn. The restaurant participates in AGA's Dine-Around program. ⊠*J. E. Irausquin Blvd. 230, Palm Beach* ☎297/586–5365 ⊕*www.moombabeach.com* ⊟*AE, D, MC, V.*

$$$– ✕**Mr. Jazz.** *Caribbean.* Although this restaurant is located
$$$$ on the second level of a new mall near the high-rise hotels, one step inside transports diners into an upscale 1940s-era Cuban jazz club. High ceilings, a large dance floor, and a stage that features live Latin performances nightly makes for a great dining experience. Happily, the menu, which features a series of Cuban-themed dishes, shines as brightly as the period light fixtures. The ropa vieja, a skirt steak served with a *mojo* sauce (made from garlic, olive oil, and citrus) is a traditional favorite, and the tenderloin is tender enough that it can literally be cut with a fork. An earlybird option from 6 to 8 PM includes four courses for $30. The live jazz performances mean that a dinner can turn out into an evening of entertainment over cocktails, and the place is quite the popular nightspot after 10. ⊠*Pasea Herencia Mall, L.G. Smith Blvd. 382-A, 2nd fl.,Palm Beach* ☎297/586–3800 ⊕*www.mrjazzaruba.com* ⊟*AE, D, DC, MC, V* ⊘*No lunch.*

$$–$$$ ✕**Old Cunucu House.** *Caribbean.* Since the mid-1990s, executive chef Ligia Maria has delighted diners with delicious homemade meals, securing her reputation as one of Aruba's finest chefs. Try the *keshi yena* or the broiled Caribbean

lobster tail served with Thermidor cream sauce and topped with Parmesan cheese. For dessert, indulge in Spanish coffee with Tia Maria and brandy. Friday night features live entertainment, and on Saturday night you can have all the fajitas you can eat. ⊠*Palm Beach 150, Palm Beach* ☎*297/586–1666* ⊕*www.theoldcunucuhouse.com* ⊟*AE, D, MC, V* ⊙*Closed Sun. No lunch.*

$$$$ ✕**Pago Pago.** *Eclectic.* This elegant and understated restaurant at the Westin may not be the most economical place to eat on the island, but it certainly is one of the nicest. Though the restaurant has built its reputation and following on consistently great steaks, the menu also offers a variety of other excellent choices. The crab cakes served with wasabi are a sure bet, and many swear by the roasted duck. Red meat lovers may test their mettle on the 24-ounce rib eye. ⊠*Westin Aruba Resort, J. E. Irasquin Blvd. 77, Palm Beach* ☎*297/586–4466 Ext. 59* ⌁*Reservations essential* ⊕*www.westinaruba.com* ⊟*AE, DC, MC, V* ⊙*No lunch, closed Wed.*

$$$– ✕**Ruinas Del Mar.** *Caribbean.* Locally cut limestone walls,
$$$$ lush gardens, and falling water make this one of the most stylish restaurants on the island. Chef Miguel Garcia creates memorable Spanish-influenced dishes that help complete the romantic picture. If possible, try and get a seat near the torch-lighted pond, so that you can admire the black swans while dining. The Sunday champagne brunch buffet is a wonder. A 15% service charge is added to your check. ⊠*Hyatt Regency Aruba Beach Resort & Casino, J.E. Irausquin Blvd. 85, Palm Beach* ☎*297/586–1234* ⊟*AE, D, DC, MC, V* ⊙*No lunch. No dinner Sun.*

EAGLE BEACH

$$$$ ✕**Le Dôme.** *Continental.* Eleven thousand bricks were
★ imported from Antwerp to add European flair to this fine-dining spot. Four dining rooms are done in different themes, the Old World and Galerie rooms being the most atmospheric. The menu changes frequently, but scampi Le Dôme are always listed and worth ordering. The wine list includes more than 250 labels. Savor Champagne with the prix-fixe Sunday brunch. Le Dôme is an AGA VIP member. ⊠*J. E. Irausquin Blvd. 224, Eagle Beach* ☎*297/587–1517* ⌁*Reservations essential* ⊟*AE, D, MC, V* ⊙*No lunch Sat.*

WORD OF MOUTH. "If you are there on a Sunday I would highly recommend the Brunch at Le Dôme. It's basically "all you can eat"
with Champagne. It's not a buffet—you order from a restricted
menu, and the waiter serves it to you. The food is prepared
individually (with regular top-ups of Champagne), so it's a very
relaxed atmosphere. We were there for a couple of hours, but
other diners who were already eating when we arrived were
still ordering." —alya

$$–$$$ ✕**Mangos.** *Caribbean.* Hotel restaurants are often stuffy
affairs, but this is not the case at Amsterdam Manor. There
are no walls here to obscure the view of Eagle Beach, and
the food is lovingly prepared with little fussiness. The creative world menu and relaxed atmosphere attract people
from around the island, and Friday night features the popular Aruban buffet, complete with a live folkloric dance
show. ✉*Amsterdam Manor, J.E. Irausquin Blvd. 252,
Eagle Beach* ☎297/587–1492 ▭AE, D, MC, V.

★ Fodor's Choice ✕**Passions.** *Eclectic.* Every night the Amsterdam
$$$–   Manor Beach Resort transforms the stretch of Eagle Beach
$$$$ in front of the hotel into a magical and romantic on-the-beach
dining room. Tiki torches illuminate the white sand, and the
linen-covered tables are within inches of the lapping water.
Dine on imaginative dishes that are as beautiful as they are
delicious. The huge tropical watermelon salad presented in
a watermelon half is refreshing and whets the appetite with
a soothing chili heat. Described as "reef cuisine," the main
courses lean toward seafood, the standout being the Seven
Seas Parade, a sampler plate featuring fresh fish, shrimp,
and lobster. After dinner, relax with your toes in the sand
and enjoy the best show that nature has to offer over sig-
nature cocktails. ✉*Amsterdam Manor Beach Resort, J.E.
Irausquin Blvd. 252, Eagle Beach* ☎297/527–1100 or
800/932–6509 ⊕*www.amsterdammanor.com* ⌦*Reserva-
tions essential* ▭AE, D, MC, V ⊙*No lunch; closed Mon.,
Tues., and Wed.*

MANCHEBO AND DRUIF BEACHES

$ ✕**DeliFrance.** *French.* If there's a breakfast haven in Aruba,
this is it. Skip the usual hotel routine, and head over to this
popular deli for a selection of freshly baked bagels and egg
dishes galore. DeliFrance is also an excellent choice for lunch,
when you can choose from dozens of sandwiches—fillings

ranging from the comforting (ham and cheese) to the down-right unusual (steak tartare). Save room for one of the hearty desserts, such as sugar waffles with whipped cream and strawberries or French apple turnover. For java lovers, the coffee alone may be worth the trip. ⊠*Certified Mega Mall, L. G. Smith Blvd. 150, Druif Beach* ☎297/588–6006 ⊕*www. delifrance-aruba.com* ▭*AE, D, MC, V* ⊗*No dinner.*

$$$ ╳**French Steakhouse.** *Steak.* You can hear someone say "ooh-la-la" whenever a sizzling steak is served. People come here from all over the island, which means the lines are often out the door. Classical music plays in the background as the friendly staff serves hearty meat entrées, fresh tuna or grouper, and even some vegetarian dishes. A five-course prix-fixe option is available seven nights a week. This eatery participates in AGA's Dine-Around program. ⊠*Manchebo Beach Resort, J. E. Irausquin Blvd. 55, Manchebo Beach* ☎297/582–3444 ⊕*www.manchebo.com/steakhouse* ▭*AE, DC, MC, V* ⊗*No lunch.*

$$$ ╳**The Pirates' Nest.** *American.* For a relaxed meal in a world-class setting, head to the Pirate's Nest restaurant, which is right on Manchebo Beach (where it meets up with the southern end of Eagle Beach, arguably one of the most beautiful spots on the island. You can catch the sunset or dine under the stars at this romantic, low-key spot, which is part of the Bucuti Beach Resort. The unrushed service is a nice reminder that you're on vacation and need only to take in the ocean view and linger over your meal. The menu is mostly standard American cuisine, with a variety of meat, fish, and vegetarian options, but the restaurant's greatest allure is its location. For couples looking for something a bit more romantic, you can sit in a secluded hut right on the sand and choose from a prix-fixe menu that includes an appetizer; a choice of fish, chicken, or meat entrée; dessert; and complimentary bottle of champagne or wine for $120 per couple. The restaurant serves three meals a day. ⊠*Bucuti Beach Resort, L. G. Smith Blvd. 55B, Manchebo Beach* ☎297/583–1100 Ext. 114 ♙*Reservations not accepted* ▭*AE, D, MC, V.*

ORANJESTAD

$ ╳**Coco Plum.** *Eclectic.* Grab a *pastechi* (meat-, cheese-, or seafood-filled turnover) and go, or stick around to relax under the thatch-roof huts and watch life unfold along Caya Betico Croes. Locals meet here for ham or tuna sand-

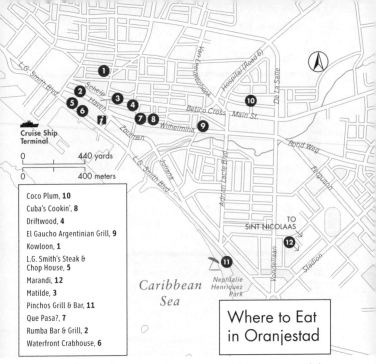

Where to Eat in Oranjestad

Coco Plum, **10**

Cuba's Cookin', **8**

Driftwood, **4**

El Gaucho Argentinian Grill, **9**

Kowloon, **1**

L.G. Smith's Steak & Chop House, **5**

Marandi, **12**

Matilde, **3**

Pinchos Grill & Bar, **11**

Que Pasa?, **7**

Rumba Bar & Grill, **2**

Waterfront Crabhouse, **6**

wiches, red-snapper platters, and chicken wings. Slake your thirst with an all-natural fruit drink in flavors such as watermelon, lemon, papaya, tamarind, and passion fruit. At the counter, order *loempias* (egg rolls stuffed with vegetables, chicken, or shrimp) or *empanas* (stuffed pockets of cornmeal). ✉*Caya Betico Croes 100, Oranjestad* 🕿*297/583–1176* ▭*No credit cards* ⊘*Closed Sun. No dinner.*

$$–$$$ ✕**Cuba's Cookin'.** *Cuban.* This funky little establishment is
★ tucked away on an innocuous street downtown. Nightly entertainment, great authentic Cuban food, and a lively crowd are the draws here. The empanadas are excellent, as is the chicken stuffed with plantains. Don't leave without trying the roast pork, which is pretty close to perfection. The signature dish is the *ropa vieja*, a sautéed flank steak served with a rich sauce (the name literally translates as "old clothes"). Service can be a bit spotty at times, depending on how busy things get. There's always a crowd, as loyal fans and fun-seekers usually crowd the bar area. ✉*Wilhelminastraat 27, Oranjestad* 🕿*297/588–0627* ⊕*www. cubascookin.com* ▭*AE, D, MC, V* ⊘*Closed Sun. mid-Apr.–mid-Dec.*

Yo, Ho, Ho, and a Cake of Rum

When Venancio Felipe Bareno came to Aruba from Spain more than a half century ago, he probably didn't think that his family's rum cake recipe would make culinary history. Now the sweet little dessert is known around the world. His nephew, Bright Bakery owner Franklin Bareno, packages the pastry for local and international sales. The history of this island favorite is printed on the side of the box. Made with Aruban Palmeira rum, Natural Bridge Aruba's rum cake makes the perfect gift for folks back home. Available in two sizes, the vacuum-sealed cakes stay fresh for up to six months. The company is registered in the United States, so you can transport the cakes through customs.

$$$–
$$$$ ✕**Driftwood.** *Caribbean.* Charming owner Francine Merryweather greets you at the door of this Aruban institution, which resembles a series of fishermen's huts. Her husband Herby sets out in his boat every morning, as he has done since the late 1980s, to bring the freshest ingredients back to the kitchen. Order his catch prepared as you like (Aruban style—panfried with a fresh tomato, vegetable, and local herbs—is best) or another of the fine fish dishes. You can't go wrong with the white sangria punch; the maître d' may even let you take home the recipe. This restaurant participates in AGA's Dine-Around program. ⊠ *Klipstraat 12, Oranjestad* ☎ *297/583–2515* ⊕ *www.driftwoodaruba.com* ⊟ *MC, V* ⊘ *Closed Tues.*

$$$–
$$$$ ✕**El Gaucho Argentine Grill.** *Steak.* Faux-leather-bound books, tulip-top lamps, wooden chairs, and tile floors decorate
☾ this Argentina-style steak house, which has been in business since 1977. The key here is meat served in mammoth portions (think 16-ounce steaks). A welcome feature is a children's playroom, which allows adults to dine while the kids are entertained with videos and games. Be warned, though: even with the kids out of sight, the noise level can still be a bit high in this busy restaurant. ⊠ *Wilhelminastraat 80, Oranjestad* ☎ *297/582–3677* ⊟ *MC, V* ⊘ *Closed Sun.*

$$ ✕**Kowloon.** *Asian.* Don't be put off by the dull exterior of this fine Asian establishment. The interior decor is tasteful and relaxing, and the combination of Indonesian and authentic Chinese is truly inspired. The most interesting items are in the EPICUREAN TOUR OF CHINA section of the menu.

Aruba's Spicy Cuisine

Arubans like their food spicy, and that's where the island's famous Madame Janette sauce comes in handy. It's made with Scotch bonnet peppers (similar to habañero peppers), which are so hot they can burn your skin when they're broken open. Whether they're turned into *pika*, a relishlike mixture made with papaya, or sliced thin into vinegar and onions, these peppers are sure to set your mouth ablaze. Throw even a modest amount of Madame Janette sauce into a huge pot of soup and your taste buds will tingle. (Referring to the sauce's spicy nature, Aruban men often refer to an attractive woman as a "Madame Janette.")

To tame the flames, don't go for a glass of water, as capsaicin, the compound in peppers that produces the heat, isn't water soluble. Dairy products (especially), sweet fruits, and starchy foods such as rice and bread are the best remedies.

The SETJU HOI SIN (the house specialty), a combination of seafood, green pepper, and black bean, is a fiery but satisfying experience. ⊠*Emmastraat 11, Oranjestad* ☎*297/582–4950* ⊕*www.kowloonaruba.com* ⊟*AE, MC, V.*

$$$–
$$$$
★
╳**L.G. Smith's Steak & Chop House.** *Steak.* A study in teak, cream, and black, this fine steak house offers some of the best beef on the island. Subdued lighting and cascading water create a pleasant atmosphere, and the view over L.G. Smith Boulevard to the harbor makes for an exceptional dining experience. The menu features quality cuts of meat, all superbly prepared. The casino is steps away, if you fancy a few pulls at the slots after dinner. ⊠*Renaissance Aruba Beach Resort & Casino, L.G. Smith Blvd. 82, Oranjestad* ☎*297/523–6115* ⊟*AE, D, MC, V* ⊗*No lunch.*

$$$–
$$$$
Fodor's Choice ╳**Marandi.** *Eclectic.* This seaside restaurant, whose name means "on the water" in Malaysian, is simultaneously cozy and chic. Everything is seductive here, from the tables placed under a giant thatched roof by the water's edge to the dining room under a palapa roof. The restaurant has moved from Oranjestad to a new location on a pier near the airport, but seems to have lost none of its charm—though the fact it is harder to find means that it is often less crowded than at its previous location. The beef cooked in local beer with foie gras, apples, and cabbage is an unusual but tasty option. Reservations are essential at any time, and if you're lucky you can dine at the chef's table,

Most Aruba restaurants are casual and fun places for a drink and a meal.

which is right in the kitchen. ✉*Bucutiweg 50, Oranjestad* ☎*297/582–0157* ⚷*Reservations essential* ⊕*www.marandi arubaa.com* ▤*AE, D, MC, V* ⊘*No lunch.*

$$$–
$$$$
★
✕**Matilde.** *French.* The venerable Chez Mathilde, once the bastion of fine French cuisine on the island, has dropped an "h" from its name and been transformed into an equally upscale but decidedly more modern eatery. The "island chic" interior and courtyard have been transformed from the belle epoque decor to a sea of crisp white- and wood-tiled walls. The menu sometimes wanders down memory lane, but tends toward Caribbean-influenced offerings such as Brie-crusted grouper served with a fruit salsa. If you are not sure about dining here, you can still sample the ambience (and watch the posers) at the trendy M lounge. ✉*Havenstraat 23, Oranjestad* ☎*297/583–9200* ⚷*Reservations essential* ⊕*www.matildearuba.com* ▤*AE, D, MC, V.*

★
$$–$$$
Fodor'sChoice ✕**Pinchos Grill & Bar.** *Eclectic.* Built on a pier, this casual spot—with only 11 tables—has one of the most romantic settings on the island. At night the restaurant glimmers from a distance, as hundreds of lights reflect off the water. Guests can watch as chef Robby Peterson prepares delectable meals on the grill in his tiny kitchen. The tuna tartare appetizer served in two spoons and accompanied by wasabi is excellent. Main courses include such favorites as skewered jumbo shrimp served with a fruit puree and grilled tenderloin cooked as you watch. Portions tend to be smaller

than is the norm in Aruba, reflecting a more European approach to meal sizes. His wife and co-owner, Anabela, keeps diners comfortable and happy. The bar area is great for enjoying ocean breezes over an evening cocktail, and there is live entertainment every weekend. ⊠ *L. G. Smith Blvd. 7, Oranjestad* ☎ *287/583–2666* ⊕ *www.interreps.nl/pinchos.htm* ⊟ *D, MC, V* ⊘ *Closed Mon. No lunch.*

$$–$$$ ✕ **Qué Pasa?** *Eclectic.* This funky eatery has moved into new digs down the street from its former address; it now serves as something of an art gallery–restaurant where diners can appreciate the colorful and funky works of local artists while enjoying a meal or savoring a drink. Outdoor spaces are a medley of terra-cotta and deep rusty hues illuminated by strings of lights. Inside, cool white prevails, letting the art stand out. Despite the name, there isn't a Mexican dish on the menu, which includes everything from sashimi to ribs; the fish dishes are especially good. Everything is done with Aruban flair, and the staff is helpful and friendly. The bar area is lively and fun. ⊠ *Wilhelminastraat 18, Oranjestad* ☎ *297/583–4888* ⊕ *www.quepasaaruba.com* ⊟ *D, MC, V* ⊘ *No lunch.*

$$–$$$ ✕ **Rumba Bar & Grill.** *Caribbean.* In the heart of Oranjestad, this lively bistro has an open kitchen where you can watch the chef prepare tasty international fare (mostly grilled seafood and beef) over a charcoal grill, with such highlights as coconut shrimp, rack of lamb, and Caribbean lobster. The presentations are fanciful, with entrées forming towering shapes over beds of colorful vegetables and sauces. You can dine on the terrace and soak up the local color or inside amid wicker and warm pink hues; the crowd is always worth watching. It's an AGA Dine-Around member. ⊠ *Havenstraat 4, Oranjestad* ☎ *297/588–7900* ⊕ *www.rumba-aruba.com* ⊟ *AE, D, MC, V* ⊘ *Closed Sun.*

$$–$$$ ✕ **Waterfront Crabhouse.** *Seafood.* Amiable, transplanted American owner Roy Leitch has created a magnet for seafood lovers in the heart of downtown. The waterfront location at the Renaissance Mall lends considerable atmosphere, as do the mural-covered walls and the live music nightly. The Alaskan king crab legs are a sure bet, and can easily serve two. Families will appreciate the extensive kids' menu, and the huge lobster tank that is bound to provide entertainment for the little ones. While most of the menu is fish-oriented, there are also several pastas as well as grilled chicken or beef for landlubbers. ⊠ *L. G. Smith Blvd.*

Where to Eat Elsewhere in Aruba

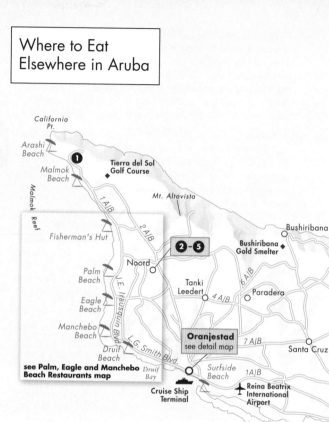

Caribbean Sea

Andicouri

ARIKOK
NATIONAL PARK

Mt. Arikok

Dos Playa

Boca Prins
(sand dunes)

Fontein
Cave

Guadikin Cave

7 A/B

Miralamar

Masiduri
Cave

Baranca Sunu

Balashi Gold
Mill Ruins

Boca
Grandi

Bachelor's
Beach

Spanish
Lagoon

Mt. Yamanota

1 B

Colorado
Pt.

1 A

1 A

Savaneta

San Nicolas

8

Natural Bridge

Mangel Halto
(Savaneta)

6 7

Santa
Largo
Beach

Grapefield
Beach

Coco's
Beach

Baby Beach

KEY
☂ Beaches

82, Oranjestad ☎*297/583–5858* ⊕*www.visitaruba.com/ waterfront* ⊟*AE, D, MC, V.*

ELSEWHERE ON ARUBA

$$$$ ✕**The Old Man & The Sea.** *Caribbean.* Local musical celebrity Jonathan Vieira and his artist mother Osyth Henriquez have created an open-air restaurant so magical that the food seems almost superfluous. Though the location in Savaneta requires a cab ride (unless you have a rental car), the setting on the beachfront, with tables in the sand, makes it well worth the effort. The menu offers both seafood and the usual steak choices, but there is a distinct Caribbean flavor to almost everything. The spicy Caesar salad and seared catch of the day coated in a spicy papaya marinade are popular choices. This is a fairly new family-run business, so service may sometimes be erratic. Still, it is hard to get too impatient with sand between your toes. Insect repellent is a must if it's been raining. ⊠*Savaneta 356A, Savaneta* ☎*297/735–0840* ⊕*www.theoldmanandthesearestaurant. com* ⊟*D, MC, V* ⊙*No lunch.*

$$–$$$ ✕**Buccaneer.** *Eclectic.* Imagine you're in a sunken ship where shark, barracuda, and grouper swim past the portholes. That's what you can find at Buccaneer, a restaurant with its own fantastic 7,500-gallon saltwater aquarium. The chefs prepare acceptable but not especially noteworthy fare. Head to this stone building flanked by heavy black chains early (around 5:45 PM) to snag a booth beside the aquarium; then order the catch of the day. AGA Dine-Around member. ⊠*Gasparito 11 C, Noord* ☎*297/586–6172* ⊕*www.buccaneer aruba.com* ⊟*AE, D, MC, V* ⊙*Closed Sun. No lunch.*

$$–$$$ ✕**Charlie's Restaurant & Bar.** *Caribbean.* Charlie's has been a San Nicolas hangout for more than 50 years. The walls and ceiling are *covered* with license plates, hard hats, sombreros, life preservers, baseball pennants, intimate apparel—you name it. The draw here is the nonstop party atmosphere—somewhere between a frat house and a beach bar. Decent but somewhat overpriced specialties include beef tenderloin and steamed shrimp in the shell. And don't leave before sampling Charlie's "honeymoon sauce" (so called because it's really hot). This may not be the ideal family outing, as it is near the town's red-light district. San Nicolas can be a bit sketchy at night, so you may prefer coming here for lunch. ⊠*Zeppenfeldstraat 56, San Nicolas*

You can dine directly on the sand at Flying Fishbone in Savaneta.

☎297/584–5086 ⊕*www.charliesbararuba.com* ▭*AE, D, MC, V* ⊘*Closed Sun.*

★ **Fodor'sChoice** ✕**Flying Fishbone.** *Seafood.* This friendly, relaxed
$$$– beach restaurant is well off the beaten path in Savaneta,
$$$$ so be sure to have a map in the car. You can dine with
your toes in the sand or enjoy your meal on the wooden
deck. The emphasis here is on fresh seafood—beautifully
presented on colorful beds of vegetables—but there are
good choices for landlubbers, too. The shrimp, shiitake,
and blue-cheese casserole is a tried and true favorite kept
on the menu to keep the regulars happy. This place pulls
a crowd year-round, so arrive early to get your table loca-
tion of choice. ⊠*Savaneta 344, Savaneta* ☎*297/584–2506*
⚓*Reservations essential* ⊕*www.flyingfishbone.com* ▭*AE,
D, DC, MC, V.*

WORD OF MOUTH. "The Flying Fishbone is ... WELL worth going to.
If you're lucky (or persistant) you'll find yourself eating right on
the sand." —dlundgren

$$–$$$ ✕**Gasparito Restaurant & Art Gallery.** *Caribbean.* You can
★ find this enchanting hideaway in a *cunucu* (country house)
in Noord, not far from the hotels there. Dine indoors,
where works by local artists are showcased on softly lighted
walls, or on the outdoor patio. Either way, the service
is excellent. The Aruban specialties—especially *pan bati*
and *keshi yena*—are feasts for the eye as well as the pal-

Chowing Down Aruban Style

With its pristine, white-sand beaches, clear blue waters, and near perfect year-round weather, Aruba is a mecca for vacationers looking for a warm getaway. The island as a whole caters to the demanding tourism industry, which has resulted in a mainly resort-food dining scene. But if you're interested in tasting something other than standard American fare—and something a bit more unique to the Dutch and Caribbean-influenced island—then you ought to try one of these local treats.

Balashi: After a day at the beach there's nothing better than sipping a nice, cold Balashi, Aruba's national beer and the only beer brewed on the island. The taste of Balashi is comparable to a Dutch Pilsner.

Bitterballen: Crispy bite-size meatballs, which are breaded and then deep-fried, make for the perfect savory snack or appetizer. Dip them in a side of mustard, and wash them down with a cold Balashi.

Bolita di Keshi: These deep-fried cheese balls are as good as they sound. They make for tasty, albeit highly caloric, appetizer.

Funchi: This classic Aruban cornmeal side dish is eaten at all times of day, and it is commonly served with soup.

Keshi Yena: A hearty, stick-to-your-ribs traditional Aruban dish of baked cheese (commonly Gouda) stuffed with chicken, spices, and raisins in a rich brown sauce.

Pan Bati: These pancakelike accompaniments are similar to funchi but slightly sweeter. As opposed to funchi, which is only made of cornmeal, pan bati is a combination of cornmeal, sugar, salt, and baking powder. It is commonly eaten as a side with a meat, fish, or soup entrée.

Pastechi: An empanadalike fried pastry filled with traditional spiced meat or cheese, served at all times of day. Although it is a favorite appetizer or snack, pastechi is also a popular breakfast item that can be found at most hotel breakfast buffets.

Saté: Marinated chunks of chicken or pork are skewered on a bamboo stick and then grilled and served with spicy peanut sauce.

ate. The standout dish is the Gasparito chicken; the sauce recipe was passed down from the owner's ancestors and features seven special ingredients, including brandy, white wine, and pineapple juice. (The rest, they say, are secret.) Gasparito is an AGA Dine-Around member. ✉*Gasparito*

Jumbo shrimp are a delicious staple at Madame Janette's.

3, Noord ☎297/586–7044 ⊕*www.gasparito.com* ▤*D, MC, V* ⊘*Closed Sun. No lunch.*

★ Fodor'sChoice ✕**Madame Janette's.** *Continental.* Named after
$$$–
$$$$
a local chili pepper (and not a local temptress), this restaurant seems haunted by the spirit of Auguste Escoffier. Calorie-counters beware: large portions and cream sauces are well represented on the menu, and hollandaise and cheese sauces abound. Presentation is an essential part of the dining experience here, and entrées rise majestically off their plates. The best part is that everything tastes as good as it looks, so those looking for a more traditional but exquisite meal will be very pleased. Try the lamb or beef rotisseries with one of the special sauces; if you're in the mood for something lighter, there are tasty salads. For an overwhelming finish, top off your meal with a sundae that billows over the edges of a massive champagne glass. Savor each course in the outdoor pebble garden, where tabletop candles cast a soft glow. With few breezes, you may feel a bit hot, and consequently a bit stuffy, in the outdoor area depending on the weather. ⊠*Cunucu Abao 37, Cunucu Abao* ☎297/587–0184 ⊕*www.madamejanette.info* ▤*AE, MC, V* ⊘*Closed Sun. No lunch.*

★ Fodor'sChoice✕**Papiamento.** *Eclectic.* The Ellis family converted
$$$–
$$$$
their 175-year-old manor into a charming bistro with an atmosphere that is elegant, intimate, and always romantic. You can feast in the dining room, which is filled with antiques,

or outdoors on the terrace by the pool (sitting on plastic patio chairs covered in fabric). The chefs mix Continental and Caribbean cuisines to produce sumptuous seafood and meat dishes. Items cooked "on the stone" are popular as much for the drama of the sizzling stone as for the incredible aromas that envelop you when they are presented. Service can be a bit slow sometimes, so don't come here if you're in a rush. ⊠ *Washington 61, Noord* 🕾 *297/586–4544* ⌖ *Reservations essential* ⊕ *www.papiamentorestaurant.com* ⊟ *AE, D, MC, V* ⊗ *Closed Mon. No lunch.*

$$$–
$$$$ ✕**Ventanas del Mar.** *Eclectic.* Floor-to-ceiling windows provide ample views across the lovely Tierra del Sol golf course and beyond to rolling sand dunes and the sea off the island's western tip. Dining on the intimate terrace amid flickering candles inspires romance. Sandwiches, salads, conch fritters, nachos, and quesadillas fill the midday menu; at night the emphasis is on seafood and meat. Crispy whole red snapper in a sweet-and-sour sauce and crab-and-corn chowder are specialties. AGA VIP member. ⊠ *Tierra del Sol Golf Course, Malmokweg* 🕾 *297/586–7800* ⊕ *www.tierradelsol.com/restaurant* ⊟ *AE, MC, V* ⊗ *Closed Mon. Apr.–Nov.*

Where to Stay

WORD OF MOUTH

"You could look at Bucuti [which] is small and on a very unpopulated beach, unlike the Hyatt [Aruba] beach, which will be very populated and busy. There is a newer hotel, the RIU Palace which is an all-inclusive hotel (Palm Beach)."

—shirleyk

"CUIDA NOS TURISTA" ("Take care of our tourists") is the island's motto, and Arubans are taught the finer points of hospitality as soon as they learn to read and write. With such cordial hosts, it's hard to go wrong no matter where you decide to stay. Accommodations in Aruba run the gamut, from large high-rise hotels and resorts to sprawling time-share condo complexes to small, locally owned boutique establishments.

Most hotels are west of Oranjestad, along L.G. Smith and J.E. Irausquin boulevards. Many are self-contained complexes, with restaurants, shops, casinos, water-sports centers, health clubs, and car-rental and travel desks. Room service, laundry and dry-cleaning services, in-room safes, minibars or refrigerators, and babysitting are standard at all but the smallest properties. Most places don't include meals in their rates, although the island now has a few all-inclusive resorts. Still, you can shop around for good dining options, as hotel restaurants and clubs are open to all island guests.

Many people prefer to stay in time-shares, returning year after year and making the island a kind of home away from home. Some time-share patrons say they like the spacious, homey accommodations and the opportunity to prepare their own meals. Note that hotel-type amenities such as shampoo, hair dryers, and housekeeping service may not be offered in time-shares; if they are, they often cost extra. Time-shares and hotels typically charge a combined total of 19% taxes and service charges on top of quoted rates, so be sure to ask about taxes before booking to avoid sticker-shock when you check out.

TYPES OF LODGINGS
Almost all the resorts are along the island's southwest coast, along L.G. Smith and J.E. Irausquin boulevards, the larger high-rise properties being farther away from Oranjestad. A few budget places are in Oranjestad itself. Since most of Aruba's beaches are equally fabulous, it's the resort, rather than its location, that's going to be a bigger factor in how you enjoy your vacation.

Large Resorts: These all-encompassing vacation destinations offer myriad dining options, casinos, shops, water-sports centers, health clubs, and car-rental desks. The island has only a handful of all-inclusives, though these are gaining in popularity.

Best Bets for Lodging

4

Fodor's offers a selective listing of quality lodging experiences, from the island's best boutique hotel to its most luxurious beach resort. Here, we've compiled our top recommendations based on the different types of lodging found on the island. The very best properties—in other words, those that provide a particularly remarkable experience—are designated in the listings with the Fodor's Choice logo.

Fodor's Choice: Amsterdam Manor Beach Resort; Aruba Marriott Resort & Stellaris Casino; Bucuti Beach Resort; Westin Aruba Resort, Spa & Casino.

Best Budget Stay: Brickell Bay Beach Club; MVC Eagle Beach; Talk of the Town Hotel & Beach Club.

Best Boutique Hotel: Amsterdam Manor Beach Resort; Bucuti Beach Resort.

Best High-Rise Resort: Aruba Marriott Resort & Stellaris Casino; Radisson Aruba Resort & Casino; Westin Aruba Resort, Spa & Casino.

Best for Honeymooners: Bucuti Beach Resort; Hyatt Regency Aruba Beach Resort & Casino; Radisson Aruba Resort & Casino.

Best for Families: Aruban Resort & Casino; Costa Linda Beach Resort; Holiday Inn Sun-Spree Mill Resort & Suites; Hyatt Regency Playa Linda Beach Resort; MVC Eagle Beach; Renaissance Aruba Resort & Casino.

Time-shares: Large time-share properties are cropping up in greater numbers, luring visitors who prefer to prepare some of their own meals and have a bit more living space than you might find in the typical resort hotel room.

Boutique Resorts: You'll find a few small resorts that offer more personal service, though not always the same level of luxury as the larger places. But smaller resorts better reflect the natural sense of Aruban hospitality you'll find all over the island.

PRICES
Hotel rates are high; to save money, take advantage of air-line and hotel packages, or visit during the summer when rates are discounted by as much as 40%. If you're traveling with kids, ask about discounts; children often stay for free in their parents' room, though there are age cutoffs.

WHAT IT COSTS IN U.S. DOLLARS				
¢	$	$$	$$$	$$$$
Hotels EP, BP, CP	under $80	$80–$150	$150–$250	$250–$350	over $350
Hotels AI	under $125	$125–$250	$250–$350	$350–$450	over $450

Prices are for two people in a standard double room in high season, excluding 8% taxes and 11% service charges.

PALM BEACH

$$–$$$ ☒ **Aruba Divi Phoenix Beach Resort.** A breathtaking location, a lively atmosphere, and comparatively reasonable rates make this hotel justifiably popular—so much so that the number of rooms was more than doubled in 2008. Most of the studio and one- or two-bedroom units have balconies with ocean views. Tropical color schemes, wood furnishings, and lots of plants make you feel at home. Coffeemakers, micro-waves, and hair dryers are among the thoughtful touches. Rooms in the newer sections feature giant flat-screen plasma TVs. Some rooms are wheelchair accessible. Sunset Beach Bistro serves breakfast, lunch, and dinner either indoors or on the beach. Work it off in the state-of-the-art fitness center. In the evening, enjoy live entertainment or try your luck at the nearby Alhambra Casino. Guests have access to the facilities of all Divi resorts on Aruba. **Pros:** great beach; small grocery store on premises; lively crowd at the beach

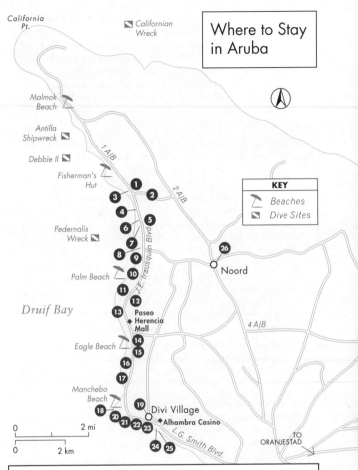

Where to Stay in Aruba

KEY

☂ Beaches
◤ Dive Sites

California Pt.

◤ Californian Wreck

Malmok Beach

Antilla Shipwreck ◤

Debbie II ◤

Fisherman's Hut

Pedernalis Wreck ◤

Palm Beach

Druif Bay

Paseo Herencia Mall

Eagle Beach

Manchebo Beach

Divi Village
◆ Alhambra Casino

Noord

L.G. Smith Blvd.

TO ORANJESTAD

1 A/B
2 A/B
4 A/B
J.E. Irausquin Blvd.

0   2 mi
0   2 km

Amsterdam Manor Beach Resort, **15**

Aruba Beach Club, **21**

Aruba Divi Phoenix Beach Resort, **13**

Aruba Marriott Resort & Stellaris Casino, **3**

Aruban Resort and Casino, **16**

Boardwalk Vacation Retreat, **1**

Brickell Bay Beach Club, **5**

Bucuti Beach Resort/Tara Suites and Spa, **18**

Casa del Mar Beach Resort, **22**

Caribbean Palm Village, **26**

Costa Linda Beach Resort, **17**

Divi Aruba Beach Resort Mega All Inclusive, **23**

Divi Dutch Village, **25**

Divi Village Golf & Beach Resort, **19**

Holiday Inn SunSpree Aruba Beach Resort & Casino, **4**

Hotel Riu Palace Aruba, **10**

Hyatt Regency Aruba, **7**

Manchebo Beach Resort & Spa, **20**

Marriott's Aruba Ocean Club, **2**

Mill Resort & Suites, **12**

MVC Eagle Beach, **14**

Occidental Grand Aruba, **8**

Playa Linda Beach Resort, **6**

Radisson Aruba Resort & Casino, **9**

Tamarijn Aruba All Inclusive Beach Resort, **24**

Westin Aruba Beach Resort & Casino, **11**

bar. **Cons:** beach can get crowded during peak times; not near major shopping areas; massive expansion has removed some of the former intimacy. ⊠*J. E. Irausquin Blvd. 75, Palm Beach* ☎*297/586–1170* ⊕*www.diviarubaphoenix. com* ↪*60 rooms, 151 1-bedroom suites, 21 2-bedroom suites, 8 3-bedroom suites* ♿*In-room: safe, kitchen, refrigerator. In-hotel: 3 restaurants, bars, pool, gym, beachfront, water sports, children's programs (ages 5–13)* ⊟*AE, D, DC, MC, V* †⊙†*EP.*

★ **Fodor's**Choice ⋐**Aruba Marriott Resort & Stellaris Casino.** The
$$$$ gentle sound of the surf and splashing waterfalls compete for your attention in this sprawling compound, where everything seems to run smoothly. A spacious lobby leads either to gardens or to a chic shopping arcade and casino. Recently renovated rooms are spacious (the largest on the island), with massive balconies; most have ocean views, and all have walk-in closets. Suites are even more expansive and have hot tubs. The restaurant choices here are unrivaled on the island, and Wave's Beach Bar is the perfect place to enjoy the sunset. **Pros:** large rooms; variety of excellent restaurants; great shopping. **Cons:** large, impersonal resort; reception can become gridlocked in peak season. ⊠*L. G. Smith Blvd. 101, Palm Beach* ☎*297/586–9000 or 800/223–6388* ⊕*www.marriott.com* ↪*413 rooms, 20 suites* ♿*In-room: safe, DVD (some), Internet, Wi-Fi. In-hotel: 7 restaurants, bars, tennis courts, pool, gym, spa, beachfront, diving, water sports, Wi-Fi, no-smoking rooms* ⊟*AE, D, DC, MC, V* †⊙†*EP.*

$$ ⋐**Boardwalk Vacation Retreat.** The owners describe this small hotel as offering "far-from-it-all tranquillity with close-to-it-all convenience." A stay here puts you only a few yards from the beach and water sports and within walking distance of casinos. Yet, despite its great location, the property manages to remain well insulated from the hustle and bustle. The suites are in separate *casitas* enveloped by gardens where hummingbirds and butterflies dart among exotic palm trees. The rooms have comfortable rattan furnishings, large living rooms and kitchens, and patios with barbecue grills and hammocks. Housekeeping is provided every other day, and laundry service is available. **Pros:** right in the middle of activities of the high-rise-area; great restaurants within walking distance; close to beach. **Cons:** no direct access to the beach; no restaurants in compound; limited views. ⊠*Bakval 20, Palm Beach* ☎*297/586–6654* ⊕*www.arubaboardwalk.com* ↪*13 units*

Associations That Accommodate

CLOSE UP

The **Aruba Hotel & Tourism Association** (☎297/582–2607 ⊕www.ahata.com ✉ahata@ setarnet.aw) was established in 1965 to maintain high standards in the tourism industry. From its original seven hotels, the organization has grown into a powerhouse of more than 80 businesses, including restaurants, casinos, stores, tour operators, and airlines. The organization's $4 million annual budget, earmarked to promote Aruba as a travel destination, comes from the Aruba Tourism Authority and from private-

sector partners. You can express opinions and register complaints on the Aruba Tourism Web site, ⊕ www.aruba.com. The organization is also involved in anti-litter efforts as part of the Aruba Limpi Committee.

Another association, the **Aruba Apartment Resort & Small Hotel Association** (☎297/582–3289), represents smaller, less expensive hotels. Members are expected to meet certain standards of accommodations and service and still offer affordable rates (often as low as $65 per night).

4

&In-room: kitchen, refrigerator, VCR. In-hotel: pool, no elevator ⊟AE, D, MC, V ⊩⌷EP.

$–$$ ⊺**Brickell Bay Beach Club.** A few minutes from the high-rise hotels and Palm Beach, Brickell Bay compensates by offering great rates. Rooms are bright with sunny exposures, though there are no ocean views. The pool area is usually lively, as is Tomato Charlie's Pizza—one of the hotel's restaurants. Golf carts ferry guests to the beach and the Excelsior Casino. Nearby are several great restaurants and the SETAR offices, where you can rent a cell phone or buy Wi-Fi access (for a lot less than most hotels charge). **Pros:** good rates for a location near the luxury resorts; complimentary breakfast; free shuttles to beach and casinos. **Cons:** no direct beach access; lacks amenities of larger properties; uninspiring views. ⊠J. E. Irausquin Blvd. 370, Palm Beach ☎297/586–0900 ⊕www.brickellbayaruba.com ⇆94 rooms, 3 suites &In-room: safe, Wi-Fi. In-hotel: 3 restaurants, bars, pool, gym, spa, some pets allowed, laundry facilities, Wi-Fi ⊟AE, D, DC, MC, V ⊩⌷EP.

$$–$$$ ⊺**Holiday Inn SunSpree Aruba Beach Resort & Casino.** This ⟲ popular, family-oriented package-tour hotel has three seven-story buildings filled with spacious rooms lining a sugary, palm-dotted shore. The pool's cascading waterfalls and sundeck, where you can enjoy the Wednesday-evening cocktail party, draws just as large a crowd as the beach. The lobby is usually overflowing with suitcases as the throngs check in and out, so don't expect too much in the way of personalized service from the front desk or the concierge at these busy times. The resort's free program for kids is a boon for families. **Pros:** affordable and predictable quality; great beachfront location; lots of activities for the kids. **Cons:** hallways have an institutional feel; lines at reception can make you feel you are back at the airport; restaurants are mediocre at best and service can be a problem. ⊠ *J. E. Irausquin Blvd. 230, Palm Beach* ☎ *297/586–3600 or 800/465–4329* ⊕ *www.aruba.sunspreeresorts.com* ⤏ *600 rooms, 7 suites* △ *In-room: refrigerator, Wi-Fi. In-hotel: 4 restaurants, bars, tennis courts, pools, gym, beachfront, diving, water sports, children's programs (ages 5–12), Internet terminal, Wi-Fi* ⊟ *AE, DC, MC, V* ⋈ *EP.*

$$$$ ⊺ **Hotel Riu Palace Aruba.** This well-situated resort reopened in August 2007 as a giant all-inclusive on the original location of the Aruba Grand Beach Resort. The white wedding cake of a resort now towers over Palm Beach with one eight-story and two 10-story towers, and has tripled the number of rooms from its days as the Aruba Grand. In keeping with the look of the Riu brand, the lobby is done in a baroque European style that feels out of place for a beach resort. Food quality is typical for an all-inclusive and not likely to inspire anyone to run home and try the recipe. With no organized activities for children, the hotel isn't family-friendly, and with large numbers of young people consuming lots of free alcohol that is probably just as well. For a hotel its size, there are few on-site programs available, though there is a casino. Rooms are either junior suites or regular doubles (doubles being carpeted), and have the signature in-room liquor dispenser of all Riu resorts. **Pros:** beautiful vistas; everything is brand-new; large and lively pool area. **Cons:** resort is very impersonal; though large, the pool area is always crowded and very loud; the à la carte restaurants all feel like sterile afterthoughts. ⊠ *J. E. Irausquin Blvd. 79, Palm Beach* ☎ *297/586–3900 or 800/345–2782* ⊕ *www.riuaruba.com* ⤏ *449 rooms* △ *In-room: safe, refrigerator. In-hotel: 5 restaurants, room service, bars, pools, gym, sauna, beachfront, water sports, Internet terminal* ⊟ *AE, D, DC, MC, V* ⋈ *AI.*

$$$$ ☐ **Hyatt Regency Aruba Beach Resort & Casino.** This 12-acre
★ resort offers everything from a casino for adults to water-
☼ slides for kids, so it's popular with families. Honeymooners
head here, too, since the resort is big enough that there are
still some quietly romantic corners. The sand-color high-rise
building is topped by a distinctive hacienda-style roof, and
interconnected pools flow through the compound and end
in an ornamental lagoon. Rooms are well equipped, but
the balconies are rather small. There's no lack of activities for adults; the resort offers horseback riding, water
sports, tennis, and a highly regarded spa. Kids' programs
are extensive as well. The restaurants are very good, most
notably Ruinas del Mar, which serves fresh seafood with
a continental flair. **Pros:** beautiful grounds; great for kids;
excellent restaurants. **Cons:** pokey balconies for such a
luxury hotel; some rooms are quite a stretch from the beach.
✉ *J. E. Irausquin Blvd. 85, Palm Beach* ☎ *297/586–1234
or 800/554–9288* ⊕ *www.aruba.hyatt.com* ⬦ *342 rooms,
18 suites* ⬦ *In-room: safe, Internet, Wi-Fi. In-hotel: 6 restaurants, room service, bars, tennis courts, pool, gym, spa,
beachfront, diving, water sports, children's programs (ages
3–12), Internet terminal* ⊟ *AE, D, DC, MC, V* ⑩*EP.*

$$$$ ☐ **Marriott's Aruba Ocean Club.** First-rate amenities and lav-
★ ishly decorated villas have made this time-share the talk
☼ of the island. Each one- and two-bedroom unit includes a
kitchen and a balcony with a spectacular ocean view. The
S-shaped pool has a swim-up bar and waterfalls, and there
are four hot tubs built into the rocks above. You can access
the facilities at the adjacent Aruba Marriott Resort & Stellaris Casino, including the spa, fitness center, and casino. An
adjacent time-share property, Marriott's Aruba Surf Club, is
just as luxurious. **Pros:** relaxed atmosphere; feels more like
a home than a hotel room; excellent beach. **Cons:** bit of a
hike to restaurants at hotel next door; pricey; attracts large
families, so kids are everywhere. ✉ *L. G. Smith Blvd. 99,
Palm Beach* ☎ *297/586–2641* ⊕ *www.marriott.com* ⬦ *311
units* ⬦ *In-room: kitchen, refrigerator, Internet. In-hotel:
restaurant, room service, pool, spa, beachfront, diving,
water sports, Wi-Fi* ⊟ *AE, D, DC, MC, V* ⑩*EP.*

$$$ ☐ **Mill Resort & Suites.** This lovely low-rise resort is deservedly
★ popular with travelers in the know. The staff is genuinely
☼ friendly and devoted to the needs of guests. Buildings are
laid out around a busy pool and bar area. The open-air
Mediterranean-style lobby has free coffee available day and
night. The resort's all-inclusive plan, which can be added

The Aruba Marriott Resort & Stellaris Casino is in the heart of Palm Beach.

onto the basic room cost, allows guests the freedom to dine off-property if they wish—although the on-site restaurant is good. Wednesday night draws a crowd from across the island for the all-you-can-eat barbecue, accompanied by live entertainment. The property is a short walk away from the beach. **Pros:** entire compound has an intimate feel; lively bar area; theme nights are fun. **Cons:** not on the beach; pool area can be busy and noisy; rates are not quite the steal they used to be. ⊠*J. E. Irausquin Blvd. 330, Palm Beach* ☎*297/586–7700* ⊕*www.millresort.com* ⋐*64 studios, 128 suites* ⌂*In-room: safe, kitchen (some). In-hotel: restaurant, bar, tennis courts, pools, gym, spa, laundry facilities, Internet terminal, Wi-Fi* ⊟*AE, D, DC, MC, V* ⓘ*EP.*

$$$–
$$$$ 🏨**Occidental Grand Aruba.** Activity surrounds the cloverleaf-shaped pool (with its waterfall and whirlpool tubs) at the heart of this all-inclusive resort. A popular place with tour groups, it always has something going on, from beer-drinking contests to bikini fashion shows. The tropical-theme rooms have white-tile bathrooms that are snug and balconies that are narrow step-outs, but better air-conditioning. The Kids' Club, which runs from 9 to 5 daily, keeps younger folks busy with a wide range of activities. The hotel has recently undergone a major renovation. **Pros:** gorgeous rooms; great beach location; wide range of activities available. **Cons:** beach and pool can get crowded, and free drinks means noise; as at most all-inclusives, the food is

lackluster; lacks any sense of personality, and feels sterile and bland overall. ✉*J. E. Irausquin Blvd. 83, Palm Beach* ☎*297/586–4500 or 800/448–8355* ⊕*www.occidentalgrand aruba.com* ⋈*398 rooms* &*In-room: safe, Wi-Fi. In-hotel: 6 restaurants, bars, tennis courts, pool, gym, beachfront, water sports, children's programs (ages 4–12), Wi-Fi* ⊟*AE, D, DC, MC, V* ⦿*AI.*

$$$– **🖾Playa Linda Beach Resort.** On one of the nicest sections of
$$$$ Eagle Beach, this lovely resort is constructed like a stepped Mayan pyramid. The design allows for maximum visibility from individual rooms and means that most balconies open to the sky (though it also means that most balconies are not entirely private and are visible from the balcony above). All units are fully equipped with kitchens—a great money-saving feature for families. Spacious studios and one- and two-bedroom suites are lavishly appointed. Frolic on the beach, dip in the free-form pool or one of the hot tubs, play a few games of tennis, or shop in the arcade. In the evening you can watch the sunset from the terrace or hit the free weekly cocktail party. Come morning, grab a quick bite at on-site Dushi Bagels. If you're looking for one of the best views on the island and a massive balcony complete with barbecue and hot tub, consider a penthouse suite. **Pros:** great beach location; tastefully decorated rooms; lots of distractions for the kids. **Cons:** Wi-Fi reception varies depending on room location; not all rooms are of the same standard, and renovation seems to be going on constantly; not as upscale as neighboring properties. ✉*J. E. Irausquin Blvd. 87, Palm Beach* ☎*297/586–1000* 🖷*297/586–5210* ⊕*www.playalinda.com* ⋈*203 units, 66 studios, 95 1-bedroom suites, 33 2-bedroom suites* &*In-room: safe, Wi-Fi, kitchen, refrigerator. In-hotel: 4 restaurants, bars, tennis courts, pool, gym, spa, beachfront, diving, water sports, laundry facilities, Wi-Fi, Internet terminal* ⊟*AE, D, DC, MC, V* ⦿*CP.*

$$$$ **🖾Radisson Aruba Resort & Casino.** Luxury is the key word at
★ this 14-acre resort. Rooms are lavishly equipped and furnished with colonial West Indian–style furniture, including four-poster beds. Large balconies overlook ocean views or tropical gardens. The pools are top-notch, and even though there's a comprehensive children's program—not to mention a large family contingent—peace and quiet are not hard to find here. The fitness center is dazzling, and the spa is the perfect place to unwind from the stresses of everyday life. **Pros:** rooms have an intimate feel; exercise

DID YOU KNOW?

Aruba has almost 8,000 hotel rooms and timeshare accommodations, most of which are lined up along Palm and Eagle beaches on the island's west coast.

Many Aruba resorts have their own spas providing body treatments and massages.

junkies will love the top-notch facilities; one of the best spas on the island. **Cons:** restaurants are good but not great; some rooms are on the small side and don't seem worth the rather high prices; you never forget you are in a big hotel. ✉ *J. E. Irausquin Blvd. 81, Palm Beach* ☎ *297/586–6555* ⊕ *www.radisson.com* ✈ *321 rooms, 32 suites* ☐ *In-room: safe, Wi-Fi. In-hotel: 4 restaurants, room service, bars, tennis courts, pools, gym, spa, beachfront, diving, water sports, children's programs (ages 5–12), laundry service, Internet terminal* ▤ *AE, D, DC, MC, V* ⦿ *EP.*

★ **Fodor's**Choice ⊠ **Westin Aruba Resort, Spa & Casino.** Westin added
$$$$ a few extra touches to the already tasteful rooms at the former Wyndham, including flat-screen TVs. The fine restaurants that helped make this hotel a standout choice in the past remain as well (in fact, aside from the logo change, it's difficult to tell the difference). Rooms, though not as large as those at some other resorts, are beautifully furnished with plentiful wood accents. The grand public spaces are always decorated with floral displays and are designed to calm. Diversions are readily available in the casino and spa; the hotel's cabaret show at the Cabaret Royale is well worth seeing even if you aren't staying here. The fact that the hotel has a "Director of Fun" and a program called "Love Your Family" is testament to their dedication to keeping guests entertained. Although it isn't cheap, the hotel offers good value for a luxury hotel by Aruba standards. **Pros:** chic and

airy rooms; magnificent beachfront and pool area; comprehensive spa facilities; great restaurants. **Cons:** immediate area is congested and busy; resort lacks an intimate feel. ⊠*J. E. Irausquin Blvd. 77, Palm Beach* ☎*297/586–4466 or 877/822–2222* ⊕*www.westinaruba.com* ⇨*481 rooms, 81 suites* ⚲*In-room: safe, Wi-Fi. In-hotel: 8 restaurants, bars, tennis court, pool, spa, beachfront, diving, water sports, Internet terminal* ⊟*AE, D, DC, MC, V* ⊚|*EP.*

EAGLE BEACH

★ **Fodor'sChoice** ☒**Amsterdam Manor Beach Resort.** An intimate, family-run hotel with a genuinely friendly staff and an authentic Dutch-Caribbean atmosphere, this little place offers excellent value for the money. The gabled mustard-yellow hotel is built around a central courtyard with a waterfall pool and wading pool. Breathtaking Eagle Beach is right across the road (guests can have lunch or dinner served on the beach). The pool bar is buzzing late into the night, and the bartender keeps everyone fully entertained. Tile-floor rooms range from small, elegantly appointed studios (some with ocean-view balconies) to two-bedroom suites with peaked ceilings and whirlpool tubs; all have kitchenettes. The restaurants serve good, reasonably priced meals, but there's a mini-grocery store on-site if you want to stock up on snacks and soft drinks. Web junkies can use the free bank of computers near reception. **Pros:** compound feels like a European village; very good family restaurant; friendly and helpful staff; recently completely renovated; prime location on Eagle Beach. **Cons:** must cross a road to reach the beach; lacks the boutiques and distractions of a larger hotel; ground-floor rooms lack privacy. ⊠*J. E. Irausquin Blvd. 252, Eagle Beach* ☎*297/527–1100 or 800/932–6509* ⊕*www.amsterdammanor.com* ⇨*68 rooms, 4 suites* ⚲*In-room: safe, DVD (some), Internet, Wi-Fi. In-hotel: 7 restaurants, bars, tennis courts, pool, gym, spa, beachfront, diving, water sports, Wi-Fi, no-smoking rooms* ⊟*AE, D, MC, V* ⊚|*EP.*

$$ ☒**Aruban Resort & Casino.** Formerly known as La Cabana, this complex of self-contained time-share units sits right across from Eagle Beach. Rooms are all newly renovated and have every imaginable home comfort, including hot tubs. A third of the suites have ocean views. Most common facilities, including the pools, are permanently crowded and usually noisy. There is an excellent children's program that

makes this a popular choice for families; those not fond of masses of children should avoid this hotel completely. **Pros:** self-catering option can be great for families; lots of distractions for the kids; rooms are colorfully decorated and cheerful. **Cons:** feels like an apartment complex; public areas are noisy and crowded; beach is across a road; ongoing renovations may be disruptive past 2009. ✉*J. E. Irausquin Blvd. 250, Eagle Beach* ☎*297/587–9000 or 800/835–7193* ⊕*www.thearuban.com* ⋑*362 suites* ♿*In-room: safe, kitchen. In-hotel: restaurant, bars, tennis courts, pools, gym, spa, diving, children's programs (ages 5–12), Internet terminal* ⊟*AE, D, DC, MC, V* ⧖*EP.*

\$\$\$\$ ⛱ **Costa Linda Beach Resort.** The name of this hotel, Spanish ☾ for "beautiful coast," speaks for itself. This paradise on earth is spread along a pristine 600-foot stretch of Eagle Beach. An inviting blue pool sits in the center of the manicured grounds. Pamper yourself with numerous amenities in the bright, spacious two-bedroom suites, which include Roman tubs and balconies overlooking the crystalline sea. Larger units also have outdoor hot tubs and barbecue grills. There are lighted tennis courts on the premises, and scuba diving, snorkeling, and boating opportunities nearby. In the evening, take a stroll to the nearby Alhambra Casino. **Pros:** beautiful location on Eagle Beach; perfect for families with many activities available; beautifully landscaped grounds. **Cons:** large resort lacks intimacy; a family favorite, so kids are everywhere; more expensive than some comparable properties in the area. ✉*J. E. Irausquin Blvd. 59, Eagle Beach* ☎*297/583–8000* ⊕*www.costalinda-aruba.com* ⋑*155 suites* ♿*In-room: kitchen, refrigerator. In-hotel: 2 restaurants, bars, tennis courts, pool, gym, children's programs (ages 5–12), laundry facilities, laundry service* ⊟*AE, MC, V* ⧖*EP.*

\$ ⛱ **MVC Eagle Beach.** For the price and the excellent location ★ across from Eagle Beach, this former vacation facility for ☾ the visiting families of Dutch marines is a great bargain. Most guests are still budget-minded Dutch tourists who can live with impeccably clean but basic and simply furnished rooms. Don't come expecting the facilities of a Hilton; however, there's a tennis court, a good restaurant serving hearty fare, and a lively bar. The hotel is also well suited to the needs of families with smaller children, as there are ample play areas and a children's pool. **Pros:** unbeatable price; popular restaurant with food at affordable prices; since the main language is Dutch, you feel that you're someplace other than South Florida here. **Cons:** spartan accommodations; not for vacationers who want to be away from kids. ⊠ *J. E. Irausquin Blvd. 240, Eagle Beach* ☎ *297/587–0110* ⊕ *www.mvceaglebeach.com* ⤳ *16 rooms, 3 suites* ⚼ *In-room: no TV. In-hotel: restaurant, bar, tennis court, pool, beachfront, laundry facilities* ▤ *MC, V* ⊚ *EP.*

MANCHEBO, PUNTA BRABO, AND DRUIF BEACHES

$$–$$$ ☒ **Aruba Beach Club.** Colonial charm and Dutch hospitality ☾ create an ambience that keeps families coming back year after year. All studios and one-bedroom units in this time-share property have pale-wood furniture, satellite TV, and a balcony, sometimes with ocean views. There's plenty to do here, including yoga and language courses in Papiamento. The front desk can arrange for water sports and other activities. Kids enjoy the playground and their own pool. A shopping arcade is filled with boutiques, a frozen-yogurt shop, and a cybercafé. If all this isn't enough, you can use the facilities at the adjoining Casa del Mar Beach Resort. The Alhambra Casino is conveniently across the street if you feel the yearning to play the slots. **Pros:** fun, family-friendly atmosphere; great beach; numerous activities; lively bars. **Cons:** pool area can be very busy; on-site restaurant is a bit pricey; hard to find a quiet spot on the grounds. ⊠ *J. E. Irausquin Blvd. 51–53, Punta Brabo Beach* ☎ *297/582–3000* ⊕ *www.arubaonline.com/beachclub* ⤳ *89 rooms, 42 suites* ⚼ *In-room: safe, Wi-Fi (some), kitchen (some). In-hotel: restaurant, bar, Internet terminal, tennis courts, spa, pool, gym, children's programs (ages 3–12), laundry service* ▤ *AE, D, DC, MC, V* ⊚ *EP.*

★ Fodor's Choice ☒ **Bucuti Beach Resort/Tara Suites & Spa.** An
$$$$ extraordinary beach setting, impeccably understated service, and attention to detail help this elegant Green Globe resort easily outclass anything else on the island. Hacienda-style buildings are surrounded by ecologically sensitive landscaping that suits the island's desertlike environment. Rooms are done in cool creams and feature cherrywood furnishings; there's a distinctly modern and European feel to the entire place. Wi-Fi is available throughout the resort. Visitors looking for the ultimate in spacious luxury would do well to choose the Tara Suites, which have unbeatable beach and sunset vistas. This hotel is very popular with return guests, so book early, as it is frequently sold out

Amsterdam Manor Beach Resort, a small hotel on Eagle Beach, is still family-run.

in high season. **Pros:** intimate European feel; impeccable service; ecoconscious hotel. **Cons:** beach can get busy, as other hotels share it; not close to any shopping, and little to buy at hotel. ⊠*L. G. Smith Blvd. 55B, Manchebo Beach* ☎*297/583–1100* ⊕*www.bucuti.com* ⤳*63 rooms, 38 suites, 3 bungalows* ♿*In-room: safe, refrigerator, Wi-Fi. In-hotel: restaurant, bars, pool, beachfront, bicycles, laundry facilities, Internet terminal, Wi-Fi* ▭*AE, D, DC, MC, V* ❢❂*CP.*

WORD OF MOUTH. "I would go back to Bucuti for the beach and the grounds but would not pay so much extra to stay in Tara Suites. Any room would probably be fine because they all face the grassy courtyard. Tara suites face the beach, but some views are obstructed." —Lina

$$ ⊡ **Casa Del Mar Beach Resort.** This beachside time-share resort offers two parts recreation, one part rest and relaxation. Deluxe accommodations are quite comfortable, with such amenities as balconies and fully equipped kitchens. Play tennis on one of four lighted courts, work out in the exercise room, arrange water sports at the activities desk, or kick back with a book from the library. You can also dine poolside at the lively Matthew's restaurant. Kids enjoy the special programs offered most weekdays from approximately 10:30 to noon. Honeymooners would be wise to look elsewhere, as this resort really does cater to families predominately. **Pros:** home-away-from-home feeling; great beach location; family-friendly. **Cons:** pool area can get crowded; kids everywhere; few quiet spots on property. ⊠*L. G. Smith Blvd. 53, Punta Brabo Beach* ☎*297/582–3000 or 297/582–7000* ⊕*www.casadelmar-aruba.com* ⋑*147 suites* ♿*In-room: safe, kitchen, refrigerator. In-hotel: restaurant, bar, tennis courts, pool, beachfront, water sports, children's programs (ages 4–10), laundry facilities* ⊟*AE, D, DC, MC, V* ⊙|*EP.*

$$$$ ⊡**Divi Aruba Beach Resort All Inclusive.** The main advantage to
☺   staying at this small resort is that it offers a variety of room types, along with the privilege of using the facilities of the adjoining Tamarijn Resort (*below*). The "Mega" concept allows guests to dine and use the facilities at other sister properties as well. Beachfront lanais offer an ideal combination of privacy and views. Because the crowd here can get quite animated—especially with free margaritas so readily available—rooms overlooking the main pool are best avoided. Children under 18 stay free when accompanied by two adults, and the kids' camp even offers Papiamento language lessons. The beach here is gorgeous; nonmotorized water sports are all included in the price, if you can drag yourself off your lounge chair. **Pros:** on wonderful stretch of beach; margarita machines in lobby; common areas feel light and airy. **Cons:** poolside area can get pretty noisy; the gourmet restaurant isn't that good; Internet access is one thing that strangely is not included. ⊠*L. G. Smith Blvd. 93, Druif Beach* ☎*297/582–3300 or 800/554–2008* ⊕*www. diviaruba.com* ⋑*203 rooms* ♿*In-room: refrigerator. In-hotel: 3 restaurants, bars, tennis court, pools, gym, beachfront, diving, water sports, bicycles, children's programs (ages 5–12), laundry service, Internet terminal* ⊟*AE, D, DC, MC, V* ⌯*3-night minimum* ⊙|*AI.*

$–$$$ ⊡**Divi Dutch Village.** Enjoy old-world ambience while basking in new-world comforts at this oceanfront time-share set around a pair of free-form freshwater pools. Many handcrafted accents adorn the Spanish-style rooms, which have kitchens and hot tubs. Larger rooms also have private patios or balconies. This is the quietest part of the Divi complex, attracting a predominately European crowd. The rates are also the cheapest of all the Divi properties, and the rooms are generally bigger—but there are no ocean views. You can participate in various outdoor activities and dine in one of several restaurants at the adjoining resorts. Kids under 15 stay free. Guests have access to the facilities of all Divi resorts on Aruba, a part of their "Mega" all-inclusive concept. **Pros:** beautiful beach is just steps away; supermarkets are within walking distance; quieter than the other Divi properties on the beach. **Cons:** not directly on the beach; no ocean views from any rooms; close to a busy intersection. ⊠*J. E. Irausquin Blvd. 47, Druif Beach* ☎*297/583–5000 or 800/367–3484* 🖷*297/582–0501* ⊕*www.dividutchvillage. com* 🖘*97 units* 🛇*In-room: kitchen, refrigerator. In-hotel: pools, beachfront, some pets allowed, no elevator* ☰*AE, D, DC, MC, V* ⅼ◎ⅼ*EP.*

$$$ 🖵**Divi Village Golf & Beach Resort.** The newest of the midsize
★   Divi resorts focuses on golf, and although it's just across the road from its sister properties, the atmosphere at this all-suites version is much quieter and more refined. Another difference is the pricing structure; base rates are not all-inclusive, though AI plans that allow you to dine at the Divi Aruba and Tamarijn are available for an additional cost. Happily, the hotel grounds are as lush and well maintained as the 9-hole golf course, and regardless of the meal plan, you get to use the facilities of all Divi resorts on Aruba. Suites are massive and include kitchens; the beach is across the road. Guests seeking the ultimate in luxury can book one of the golf villas that overlook the course and have private rooftop Jacuzzis. **Pros:** excellent golf course; spacious rooms; lushly landscaped grounds. **Cons:** bit of a hike from some rooms to the lobby; you must cross a busy road to get to the beach. ⊠*J. E. Irausquin Blvd. 93, Druif Beach* ☎*297/583–5000* ⊕*www.divivillage.com* 🖘*250 suites* 🛇*In-room: kitchen, Internet, Wi-Fi. In-hotel: 3 restaurants, room service, bars, golf course, tennis courts, pools* ☰*AE, D, DC, MC, V* ↻*3-night minimum* ⅼ◎ⅼ*EP.*

$$–$$$ 🖵**Manchebo Beach Resort & Spa.** Amid 100 acres of gardens, this resort feels miles away from it all; in reality it's five minutes from town and across from a complex with shops, restaurants, and a casino. Rooms are decorated with blond-wood furnishings and bright floral fabrics and are equipped with coffeemakers. Guests who choose to purchase the all-inclusive package are treated to à la carte breakfast at the poolside Garden Terrace, lunch at the Pega Pega restaurant, dinner at the French Steakhouse (famous for Argentina-style steaks), and unlimited house drinks at the bar. A pavilion on one of the prettiest stretches of Eagle Beach is the site of many weddings. A new spa is proving popular with both guests and outside clients. **Pros:** great beach location; nearby casino; good on-site restaurant. **Cons:** lacks

The beachfront at Bucuti Beach Resort.

some of the amenities of a larger resort; beach area can get crowded. ⊠*J. E. Irausquin Blvd. 55, Manchebo Beach* ☎*297/582–3444 or 800/223–1108* ⊕*www.manchebo.com* ↪*71 rooms* ☝*In-room: safe, refrigerator. In-hotel: 2 restaurants, bars, spa, pool, beachfront, water sports, Internet terminal, Wi-Fi* ☐*AE, D, DC, MC, V* Ⓞ|*AI, EP.*

WORD OF MOUTH. "The staff at the Manchebo is what makes the resort shine. We had the same maid all week. She got to know us and smiled and waved at us each morning when we went to breakfast. Ignacio is the bartender at the Pega Pega bar in the evenings. He was very personable and made us laugh. We went to the bar most evenings if we didn't go out at night." —travelenthusiast

$$$
$$$$ ☲Tamarijn Aruba All Inclusive Beach Resort. An upscale alternative to its sister property, the Divi Aruba Beach Resort (*above*), this resort is pleasantly laid-back for an all-inclusive. Guests seeking additional excitement can take a short walk along the beach to the more rambunctious sister property next door. All rooms are oceanfront and feature blond-wood furnishings and ample balconies. Guests looking for more space can choose the newly added suites, which are in the Divi Dutch Village part of the complex (*above*). The rate covers food, beverages, entertainment, an array of activities, and even tickets to the weekly Bon

Bini Festival. Parents will appreciate the special discount offered on an extra room for the kids. A free shuttle runs to the Alhambra Casino until 3 AM. **Pros:** stunning beach; access to the Divi Aruba Beach Resort next-door; perfect for families. **Cons:** being right on the beach can mean noise during busy periods; the linear layout means some rooms are quite far from the lobby. ⊠*J.E. Irausquin Blvd. 41, Druif Beach* ☎*297/525–5200 or 800/554–2008* ⊕*www. tamarijnaruba.com* ⬳*236 rooms, 97 suites* ♿*In-hotel: 3 restaurants, bars, tennis courts, pools, gym, beachfront, water sports, bicycles, Internet terminal* ⊟*AE, D, DC, MC, V* ⬳*3-night minimum* ⵙ*AI.*

NOORD

$$ ⵟ**Caribbean Palm Village.** Lush gardens lend an air of tranquillity to this tile-roof resort not far from Palm Beach. Some of the one- and two-bedroom accommodations have fully equipped kitchens; all have private balconies. Eat breakfast or lunch at the pool bar, then swim a few laps or serve up a few aces on the tennis court. The hotel, a short walk from restaurants, casinos, and nightclubs, generally attracts people over 30. Eagle Beach is a 10-minute walk from the resort, and free shuttle buses depart for the sand weekdays at 9:25 and 2:25, returning at 12:30 and 4. Valentino's, one of the best restaurants on the island, is in the compound. **Pros:** excellent for families; good security on site; lively pool area. **Cons:** no beach; some rooms feel dated; laid-back atmosphere might be a bit too quiet for younger adults without children. ⊠*Palm Beach Rd., Noord 43E, Noord* ☎*297/586–2700* ⊕*www.cpvr.com* ⬳*170 rooms* ♿*In-room: kitchen, Wi-Fi (some), refrigerator. In-hotel: restaurant, bar, Wi-Fi, tennis court, pools* ⊟*AE, DC, MC, V* ⵙ*EP.*

ORANJESTAD

$$$–
$$$$
★ ⵟ**Renaissance Aruba Resort & Casino.** This downtown hotel has two distinct parts: the Renaissance Marina Hotel and the Renaissance Ocean Suites. Standard rooms are in the Marina section, which is on Oranjestad's main drag and overlooks the harbor. The Ocean Suite rooms are larger and have separate living areas and kitchenettes. The main hotel pool actually juts out 25 feet above L.G. Smith Boulevard (swimmers can look down on the street). Rooms here are spacious and well appointed; some overlook the six-floor

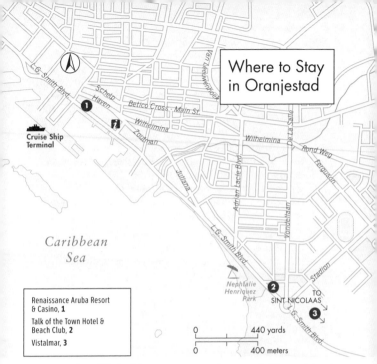

Cruise Ship Terminal

Caribbean Sea

Renaissance Aruba Resort & Casino, **1**

Talk of the Town Hotel & Beach Club, **2**

Vistalmar, **3**

TO SINT NICOLAAS

0	440 yards
0	400 meters

atrium filled with restaurants and stores. A 40-acre island just offshore has the only private beaches in Aruba, and is reserved for hotel guests (the boat to the island leaves from the hotel lobby). Most restaurants in the attached Renaissance Seaport Mall allow diners to sign for their meals. **Pros:** right in the heart of the downtown shopping district; lobby and shopping areas are always lively; pool area offers an unmatched view of the port. **Cons:** rooms overlooking the atrium can be a bit claustrophobic; beach is off-site, hard to find a quiet spot. ⊠*L. G. Smith Blvd. 82, Oranjestad* ☎*297/583–6000 or 800/421–8188* ⊕*www. renaissancearuba.com* ⤳*287 rooms, 269 suites* ⌂*In-room: kitchen (some), Internet. In-hotel: 5 restaurants, room service, bars, tennis court, pools, gym, spa, beachfront, diving, water sports, children's programs (ages 5–12), laundry facilities, Internet terminal, Wi-Fi, no-smoking rooms* ⊟*AE, D, DC, MC, V* ⊙*EP.*

$–$$ ⊡**Talk of the Town Hotel & Beach Club.** This property offers excellent rates and a fairly convenient location—it's a 10-minute walk from downtown. The facilities are built around a courtyard with a large, palm-fringed pool. Free Wi-Fi throughout the property is a rarity on Aruba, and should keep Web junkies happy. Rooms are bright and airy (some include kitchenettes), and all have a view of the pool. The Moonlight Patio Bar & Grill restaurant just off the lobby offers reasonably priced meals. Surfside beach is across the road—but be careful as you cross the busy thoroughfare. **Pros:** great value for money; close to main shopping area; free breakfast included with most room rates. **Cons:** not exactly luxurious; on a busy street; pool could use some work, but is serviceable. ⊠*L. G. Smith Blvd. 2, Oranjestad* ☎*297/582-3380* ☎*297/583-2446* ⊕*www. tottaruba.com* ⤸*63 rooms* ⚲*In-room: safe, kitchen, refrigerator, Wi-Fi. In-hotel: restaurant, bar, pool, Wi-Fi, laundry service* ⊟*AE, MC, V* ⎮⊙⎮*EP.*

$–$$ ⯐**Vistalmar.** Alby and Katy Yarzagary converted this property across the street from the fishing pier in Oranjestad into a homey inn. Simply furnished one-bedroom apartments each have a full kitchen, a living-dining area, and a sunny porch. The Yarzagarys provide snorkeling gear and stock arriving guests' refrigerators with breakfast fixings. There's no beach at this spot south of town, but the sea is just across the street. The major drawback is the distance from shopping and dining options, but it's only five minutes from the airport. **Pros:** charming and intimate; rates allow for up to four adults and kids; impeccably clean. **Cons:** not near major shopping area; no beach. ⊠*Bucutiweg 28, Oranjestad* ☎*297/582-8579* ⊕*www.arubavistalmar.com* ⤸*8 rooms* ⚲*In-room: kitchen, Wi-Fi. In-hotel: laundry facilities* ⊟*D* ⎮⊙⎮*CP.*

Nightlife and the Arts

WORD OF MOUTH

" One of the main reasons that we returned to Aruba was to relive a favorite vacation memory—Kukoo Kunuku. If you like to dance and drink and have a good time, you'll enjoy it too."

—travelenthusiast

THEY PUMP UP THE VOLUME at Aruba's resort bars when the sun sets. Unlike many other islands, nightlife here isn't confined to touristy folkloric shows. In addition to spending time in one of the many casinos, you can slowly savor a drink while the sun dips into the sea, dance to the beat of a local band, bar-hop in a colorful bus, or simply stroll along a deserted starlit beach.

Arubans like to party—the more the merrier—and they usually start celebrating late in the evening. The action, mostly on weekends, doesn't pick up until around midnight. Casual yet trendy attire is the norm. Most bars don't have a cover charge, although most nightclubs do. Bigger clubs, such as Club Havana, may have lines on weekends, but they move quickly; use this time to start your socializing, and you may just end up with a dance partner before you even set foot inside the door. Drink specials are available at some bars, and every establishment will gladly give you a free Balashi cocktail (the local term for a glass of water). Both bars and clubs have either live bands or DJs, depending on the night.

No matter where you choose to party, be smart about getting back to your hotel. Drinking then driving, of course, is against the law. If you're within walking distance, go ahead and hoof it. Taxis are a good option if your hotel is farther away. The island is safe, and you'll probably wander with swarms of other visitors in town and along Palm Beach.

NIGHTLIFE

For information on specific events, check out the free magazines *Aruba Nights, Aruba Events, Aruba Experience,* and *Aruba Holiday,* all available at the airport and at hotels.

BARS

Alfresco Lobby Bar (⊠*Hyatt Regency Aruba Beach Resort & Casino, J.E. Irausquin Blvd. 85, Palm Beach* ☎297/586–1234 Ext. 4265) offers you a glimpse of the elaborate swimming pool with whirlpools, waterslides, and waterfalls from the Hyatt Regency Aruba Beach Resort & Casino's lovely lobby bar. This is where guests gather to hear live music early in the evening and stop by for a nightcap after the casino closes.

Bambu (⊠*Babijn 53, Paradera* ☎*No phone*) is a local joint that offers typical Aruban food, cheap drinks, and a lively crowd on the terrace on weekends.

CLOSE UP

A Bartender's Life

For some people, tending bar is a job. But for Tariq Ohab, one of Aruba's most popular bartenders, it's a way of life. Born in Aruba, the islander has a passion for mixing cocktails and everything that goes along with it. "If I could have any bartending job in the world," he says, "I'd like to stay right here."

Ohab lived in the United States for about eight years, but eventually moved back to the island he loves—a fact that endears him to his local clients, who appreciate his knowledge of Aruban culture and tales of his travels. Ohab recalls swapping small-world stories with a couple from Spokane who were surprised to find he had once lived in Olympia. "I meet a lot of interesting people," he says. "Most of the people I meet are always ready to start a conversation and chat up a storm."

Café Bahia, a popular watering hole, has been Ohab's habitat for the past eight years. Although most of his clients are tourists trying to take their minds off their sunburns, plenty of celebrities drop by for a cold one. Baseball player Sidney Ponson, a native of Aruba, is a regular. One day O. J. Simpson himself paid a visit. "He ordered orange juice," says Ohab, "and that's no joke."

Ohab especially enjoys mixing up Café Bahia's specialty drinks. The best bang for the buck, according to Ohab, is called the Blackout. "It's the strongest drink we have," he says. "It's made with five shots: tequila, whiskey, amaretto, 151, and Southern Comfort. It's topped with cranberry juice; then we mix in some blue grenadine, and it becomes black before your eyes." Served in a big glass, the concoction takes an average person about an hour to finish. Most customers, he adds, don't stop at just one.

It may sound like Ohab's life is one big party, but he has a mellower side as well. On Sunday, his day off, you can find him at home with his wife and two kids. "Since my job is so social, I go out every night of the week," he says. "On Sundays, it's all about the family."

5

The beachfront **Bugaloe** (⊠*Palm Beach, near Riu Palace* ☎*297/586–2050*) is usually full of beauties in skimpy bathing suits and windsurfers in baggy shorts. There's live local music on Friday and Sunday, with everything from reggae and salsa to pop.

Charlie's Bar (⊠*Zeppenfeldstraat 56, San Nicolas* ☎*297/584–5086*) has been an Aruba institution since 1941. It's a bit far from most hotels, but certainly worth the trip. Expect

CLOSE UP

Brewing Up Something Special

There was a time when you could walk into any bar in Aruba and get a glass of water by asking for a Balashi Cocktail. (The name came from the fact that the desalination plant is in an area known as Balashi.) Since the creation of Balashi, the first locally brewed beer, such a drink order has taken on a whole new meaning.

Made by a German brewmaster in a state-of-the-art facility using only the finest hops and malt, Balashi is golden-color pilsner. The beer is a source of local pride, even more so since it won the prestigious Monde Selection at an international competition in 2001. Visitors love it as well. "It's a big tourist thing," explains Gerben Tilma, general manager of the plant. "Everyone wants to know what the best local products are. Now we can tell them."

The **Balashi Brewery** (⊠ *Balashi* ☎ *297/585–4805*) has a free one-hour tour at 10 AM daily. There's also a souvenir shop, a café, and a 10,000-square-foot beer garden where you can enjoy a cold one.

a raucous (and, most likely, very inebriated) crowd. The food here is quite good as well, all the better for padding your stomach before the margaritas.

WORD OF MOUTH. "A visit to Charlie's Bar, which is in [San Nicolas]—you will need a car to get there as it is near Baby Beach." —paris350

Cheta's Bar (⊠ *Paradera 119, Paradera* ☎ *297/582–3689*), which has been in business since 1948, is a real locals' joint and holds no more than four customers at a time. There aren't any bar stools, either, which is why most patrons gather out front.

★ You can watch the crowds from the terrace at **Choose a Name** (⊠ *Havenstraat 36, Oranjestad* ☎ *297/588–6200*) or climb up on the bar for your karaoke debut; bands also perform several nights a week.

Coco Beach Bar & Grill Restaurant (⊠ *Coco's Beach, Seroe Colorado* ☎ *297/584–3434*) is a popular spot for food and drinks any time of the day or night.

Cuba's Cookin' (⊠ *Wilhelminastraat 27, Oranjestad* ☎ *297/588–0627*) always has a lively crowd. The cozy place is also a restaurant serving great ethnic food. On weekends the

Aruba is one of the Caribbean's nightlife centers.

bar is packed with people who come to enjoy live Cuban music, and the dancing goes on until the wee hours of the morning.

For specialty drinks, try **Iguana Joe's** (✉ *Royal Plaza Mall, L. G. Smith Blvd. 94, Oranjestad* ☎ *297/583–9373*). The creative reptilian-theme decor is as colorful as the cocktails.

★ With painted parrots flocking on the ceiling, **Mambo Jambo** (✉ *Royal Plaza Mall, L. G. Smith Blvd. 94, Oranjestad* ☎ *297/583–3632*) is daubed in sunset colors. Sip one of several concoctions sold nowhere else on the island, then browse for memorabilia at a shop next door.

With front-row seats to view the green flash—that ray of light that supposedly flicks through the sky as the sun sinks into the ocean—the **Palms Bar** (✉ *Hyatt Regency Aruba Beach Resort & Casino, J.E. Irausquin Blvd. 85, Palm Beach* ☎ *297/586–1234*) is the perfect spot to enjoy the sunset.

Señor Frog's (✉ *Weststraat 1, Oranjestad* ☎ *297/582–0355*) is near the building that once housed the popular (but now closed) Carlos & Charlie's and owned by the same parent company in Mexico. This hot spot pulls the same wild crowd as its predecessor. The music is loud, and the crowd is pumped up by animated staff and such alcoholic favorites as the yard of beer. If beer is not your thing, take comfort in knowing you can also buy a yard of margarita. Either way you can take the glass home with you. Anyone looking to enjoy the thrill of the waterslide that runs from the upstairs bar and ends in a landing pool on the balcony should bring a bathing suit. Definitely an essential stop for the younger partying set.

Sunset Bar (⊠ *La Cabana All Suite Beach Resort & Casino, J. E. Irausquin Blvd. 250, Eagle Beach* ☎297/587–9000) serves cocktails at a swim-up bar.

★ **Tequila Aruba** (⊠ *Weststraat 3, Oranjestad* ☎297/588–7076) has replaced the venerable Carlos & Charlie's, and for some it was a sad day when the famous bar closed its doors, but this establishment at the same location seems to be attracting just as many partiers. The drink of choice here is tequila, and every night features a different theme. Wednesday is ladies night, when visitors and locals alike come to gawk at the scantily clad male dancers.

CRUISES

You can take a Sunset Happy Hour Cruise aboard the 80-foot sailing vessel **Mi Dushi** (☎297/586–2010 ⊕*www. midushi.com*), where you can enjoy Caribbean snacks as you toast with champagne. The open-air bar serves premium brands (included in your ticket price). Cruises depart Wednesday and Friday at 5 PM from the De Pal Pier between the Riu Palace and the Radisson, returning about 7 PM. The cost is $30 per person.

Don't be surprised if you're enjoying a romantic ocean-view dinner on Palm Beach and see a twinkle of lights on the horizon. It may be the **Tattoo** (☎297/586–2010 ⊕ *www. arubatattoo.com*), a catamaran operated by Aruba Adventures that sails every night except Sunday from 8 to midnight. There are three decks for dancing (with live bands and a DJ), dining, and stargazing. End the evening with the famous rope swing and waterslide. The cost is $49 per person. Just be aware that the food is not really great, and if you aren't enjoying the experience you don't have much choice but to wait it out.

DANCE AND MUSIC CLUBS

★ Popular with locals and tourists, **Café Bahia** (⊠ *Weststraat 7, Oranjestad* ☎297/588–9982) draws a chic crowd every Friday for happy hour. If you come for dinner, stick around for drinking and dancing as the music heats up. On Tuesday night a band from one of the cruise ships plays local favorites.

A sunset happy hour cruise is a popular pastime.

Hot spot **Club Havana** (⊠*L. G. Smith Blvd. 2, Oranjestad* ☎*297/582–0152*) has a happy hour every Friday night until 2 AM. Two local bands jam live on Saturday from 10 PM to 4 AM.

Euphoria (⊠*Royal Plaza Mall, L. G. Smith Blvd. 94, Oranjestad* ☎*297/588–9450*) keeps its energy level undiminished until closing time. Every night a young crowd raves the night away.

La Fiesta (⊠*Aventura Mall, Plaza Daniel Leo, Oranjestad* ☎*297/583–5896*) is a nonstop party that attracts a casual yet classy crowd. Inside, heavy red curtains add drama. Although there's no dance floor, a cool mix of music inspires patrons to bop at the bar.

★ For jazz and other types of music, try cozy **Garufa Cigar & Cocktail Lounge** (⊠*Wilhelminastraat 63, Oranjestad* ☎*297/582–582-3677*), which serves as a lounge for customers awaiting a table at the nearby Gaucho Argentine Grill (you're issued a beeper so you know when your table is ready). While you wait, have a drink, enjoy some appetizers, and take in the leopard-print carpet and funky bar stools. The ambience may very well draw you back for an after-dinner cognac. There's live entertainment most nights, and the powerful smoke extractor system helps make life bearable for nonsmokers.

Bar-Hopping Buses

CLOSE UP

A couple of bus operators can turn a regular evening out on the town into a whirlwind tour of the island's hottest nightspots. One uniquely Aruban institution is a psychedelically painted '57 Chevy bus called the **Kukoo Kunuku** (☎297/586–2010 ⊕www.kukookunuku.com). On weeknights you can find as many as 40 passengers traveling between half a dozen bars from sundown to around midnight. The $59 fee per passenger includes dinner, some drinks, and picking you up (and pouring you out) at your hotel. Group and private charter rates are available. Needless to say, reservations are essential. **Banana Bus** (⊕www.bananabusaruba.com) offers a similar experience—minus dinner—in a bus with a 20-foot banana mounted on the roof. Five drinks are included in the $45-per-person price. Reservations can be made at your hotel front desk, and the bus will pick you up there as well.

Gilligan's (⊠*Radisson Aruba Caribbean Resort, J. E. Irausquin Blvd. 81, Palm Beach* ☎*297/586–6555*), the beachside bar at the Radisson resort, always puts local bands in the spotlight. You'll feel like you've been shipwrecked on an uncharted tropical isle as you sip cocktails at the bar.

At **Pata Pata** (⊠*La Cabana All Suite Beach Resort & Casino, J. E. Irausquin Blvd. 250, Eagle Beach* ☎*297/587–9000*) on busy Eagle Beach, musicians take to the stage every evening at.

Live music every evening makes **Pelican Terrace** (⊠*Divi Aruba Beach Resort, J. E. Irausquin Blvd. 45, Druif Beach* ☎*297/582–3300*) a popular nightspot. Sip creative cocktails, dance around the pool, and grab a late-night snack—perhaps a pizza that's piping hot from the wood-burning oven. Liveliness is guaranteed, as most of the other patrons are resort guests enjoying all-inclusive drinks.

Local bands alternate sets at **Rick's Café** (⊠*Westin Aruba Beach Resort & Casino, J. E. Irausquin Blvd. 77, Palm Beach* ☎*297/586–4466*), a popular watering hole. The bar is inside the Westin's casino, so you can throw a quarter in the slots on your way in—you just might win enough to cover your bar tab.

At the Marriott's **Stellaris Lounge & Lobby Bar** (⊠*Aruba Marriott Resort & Stellaris Casino, L. G. Smith Blvd. 101, Palm*

Aruba has several art galleries where you can buy original paintings.

Beach ☎297/586–9000) local bands gets the party started about 9 PM and keep it going until at least 2 AM.

THEME PARTIES

At last count there were more than 50 theme nights offered during the course of a week. Each party features a buffet dinner, dancing, and entertainment (often of the limbo, steel-band, stilt-walking variety). For a complete list contact the Aruba Tourism Authority.

The fun Carnival-theme show at the **Aruba Marriott** (⊠*L. G. Smith Blvd. 101, Palm Beach* ☎297/586–9000) should not be passed up just because it's at a hotel. It's done every Tuesday night.

Holiday Inn Sunspree (⊠*J. E. Irausquin Blvd. 230, Palm Beach* ☎297/586–3600) lets you get your limbo on at its Wednesday-night party.

THE ARTS

Puerto Rico has Ricky Martin, Jamaica has Bob Marley, and Aruba has—well, Aruba has a handful of stars who aren't quite as famous but are just as talented. Over the years, several local artists, including composer Julio Renado Euson (who once won a competition against Ricky Martin), choreographer Wilma Kuiperi, sculptor Ciro Abath, and visual artist Elvis Lopez, have gained international renown. Further, many Aruban musicians play more than one type

DID YOU KNOW?

The Kukoo Kunuku always starts with a Champagne toast at the California Lighthouse followed by dinner and bar-hopping until midnight. It's one of the most popular nightlife activities in Aruba.

Cool Concoctions

CLOSE UP

These drink recipes come from Aruban-born bartender Clive Van Der Linde.

■ **The Wow.** Mix equal parts (2 ounces or so) of rum and vodka as well as triple sec, a splash of tequila, grenadine, coconut cream, and pineapple and orange juice. Quips Van Der Linde, "You won't taste the alcohol, but after two, you'll feel pretty good."

■ **The Iguana.** Mix equal parts of rum and vodka, and add either blue Curaçao or blue grenadine for color. Add crème de banana liqueur, coconut cream, and pineapple juice. Says Van Der Linde, "I learned this one more than 10 years ago on the first sailing boat I worked on. It was called the *Balia*, which means 'to dance.'"

■ **The Captain's Special.** Mix equal parts of rum and vodka, and add a splash of amaretto, crème de banana, and pineapple and orange juice. "It's really simple," says Van Der Linde. "Just blend with crushed ice and it's ready to drink."

of music (classical, jazz, soca, salsa, reggae, calypso, rap, pop), and many compose as well as perform.

The Union of Cultural Organizations is devoted to developing local art while broadening its international appeal. UNOCA provides scholarships to help artists of all ages to participate in exhibitions, shows, and festivals. Although some internationally recognized stars have returned to Aruba to help promote the island's cultural growth, renowned conductor and pianist Eldin Juddan says the island needs to do more to promote local musicians. "There's a lot of talent, but professional guidance is needed to bring these talents and music to their potential."

The **Cas Di Cultura** (✉ *Vondellaan 2, Oranjestad* ☎ *297/582– 1010*), the island's cultural center, continuously hosts art exhibits, folkloric shows, dance performances, and concerts. Further, the island's many festivals showcase arts and culture. To find out what's going on, check out *Aruba Today,* the local newspaper, or *Calalou,* a Caribbean publication dedicated to the visual arts. You can also phone the national library, which has a bulletin board of events.

CLOSE UP

In Tune with Jonathan Vieira

His parents were always traveling, so when musician Jonathan Vieira was growing up he often stayed with his grandmother. He was fascinated with her old piano. He hit his first note when he was four, and has been playing ever since. The Aruba native, who taught himself to play, recorded an album called *Two Generations* with Padu del Caribe, one of the composers of the island's national anthem. Vieira speaks highly of his collaborator, calling him the "father of our culture."

"On Aruba, people need to have more of an awareness of cultural music," Vieira says. "The popular stuff catches on quick; we have to have a balance."

Many of his own musical creations show his affinity for local rhythms, though he also is well versed in classical and contemporary music.

When he was about 14, a local promoter heard about his talents and invited him to open one of the concerts she was organizing. The reaction was positive, and for the first time Vieira realized he could use his talent to make some money—or at least pay his school expenses. At age 17, Vieira headed to the United States to continue his education. He attended the Berkeley College of Business in New York City, where he earned a degree in information management systems. It was his third degree; the others are in film and video production and recording arts production. "On the island," says Vieira, "everyone knows me as a pianist."

Although his first love is music, Vieira has also been dabbling in film. "I have been doing a bit of acting recently to try it out," he says. In the meantime, Vieira is busy giving back to the island he calls home. He has opened a new beach restaurant, The Old Man and The Sea, in collaboration with his mother and is spending much more time on the island. Vieira gives chamber concerts at the Access, an art gallery and performance space in Oranjestad. He also invites other artists to join him in special holiday performances.

ART GALLERIES

★ **Access** (⊠*Caya G. F. Betico Croes 16–18, Oranjestad* ☎297/ *588–7837*) showcases new and established artists; it's a major venue for Caribbean art. Located in the downtown shopping district, the gallery is home to a thriving cultural scene that includes poetry readings, chamber music concerts, and

Carnival

Aruba's biggest bash incorporates local traditions with those of Venezuela, Brazil, Holland, and North America. The festival was introduced to the island by Trinidadians who had come to work at the oil refinery in the 1940s. In Aruba, Carnival consists of six weeks of jump-ups (traditional Caribbean street celebrations), competitions, parties, and colorful parades. The celebrations culminate with the Grand Parade held in Oranjestad on the Sunday before Ash Wednesday. It lasts for hours and turns the streets into one big stage. The two main events are the Grand Children's Parade, where kids dress in colorful costumes and decorate floats, and the Lightning Parade, consisting of miles of glittery floats and lavish costumes. Steel-pan and brass bands supply the music that inspires the crowds to dance. All events end on Shrove Tuesday: at midnight an effigy of King Momo (traditionally depicted as a fat man) is burned, indicating the end of joy and the beginning of Lenten penitence.

screenings of feature films and documentaries. The owner, artist Landa Henriquez, is also a bolero singer.

At **Galeria Eterno** (⊠*Emanstraat 92, Oranjestad* ☎*297/583–9607*) you can find local and international artists at work. Be sure to stop by for concerts by classical guitarists, dance performances, visual-arts shows, and plays.

Galeria Harmonia (⊠*Zeppenfeldstraat 10, San Nicolas* ☎*297/584–9484*), the island's largest exhibition space, has a permanent collection of works by local and international artists.

Gasparito Restaurant & Art Gallery (⊠*Gasparito 3, Noord* ☎*297/586–7044*) features a permanent exhibition by Aruban artists.

★ **Insight Art Studio** (⊠*Paradera Park 215, Paradera* ☎*297/582–5882*) hosts exhibitions of local and international artists. Don't expect to find the usual paintings of pastel-color skies. Owner Alida Martinez, a Venezuelan-born artist, likes more avant-garde displays. Her own mixed-media creations juxtapose erotic and religious themes. The space, which includes a studio, is a magnet for the island's art community. Viewing is by appointment only.

FESTIVALS

ANNUAL EVENTS

The **Aruba Music Festival,** a two-day event held in September or October, features international pop stars. (Sure, the artists may not have current hits, but the festival can be a fun nostalgic experience.) Past performers include Peter Frampton; REO Speedwagon, Gloria Estefan, and Pat Benatar.

★ New Year's Eve is a big deal in most places, but on Aruba the fireworks that light up the sky at midnight are just the beginning. **The Dande Stroll** continues throughout New Year's Day. Groups of musicians stroll from house to house, singing good-luck greetings for the New Year. A prize is awarded to the group with the best song, which is sung by islanders during the next 12 months. Dande, by the way, comes from the Papiamento word "dandara," which means "to have a good time."

The **Hi-Winds Pro Am Windsurfing Competition** brings windsurfers of all skill levels from more than 30 different countries during June or July to compete off the beaches at Fisherman's Huts at Hadikurari.

The **International Dance Festival Aruba** draws dance companies from the Caribbean, the United States, and Europe each October to participate in workshops, lectures, demonstrations, and exhibitions.

International Theatre Festival Aruba is held every other October. Theater groups from around the world perform 45- to 70-minute shows at the Cas Di Cultura.

Aruba's **Jazz and Latin Music Festival** is held each June, when for a few nights you can hear jazz and Latin music performed at the outdoor venue next to the Renaissance Aruba Beach Resort at Renaissance Mall.

National Anthem & Flag Day, an official holiday, is on March 18. On this day you can stop by Plaza Betico Croes in Oranjestad for folkloric presentations and other traditional festivities.

St. John's Day—also known as Dera Gai, the annual "burying of the rooster" festival—is celebrated June 24, the Feast of St. John the Baptist. Festive songs, bright yellow-and-red costumes, and traditional dances mark this holiday dating from 1862. Today, the rooster—which symbolizes a successful harvest—has been replaced by a gourd.

The Bon Bini Festival folkloric festival is held weekly.

WEEKLY PARTIES

★ The **Bon Bini Festival,** a year-round folkloric event (the name means "welcome" in Papiamento), is held every Tuesday from 6:30 PM to 8:30 PM at Fort Zoutman in Oranjestad. In the inner courtyard you can check out the Antillean dancers in resplendent costumes, feel the rhythms of the steel drums, browse among the stands displaying local artwork, and partake of local food and drink. Admission is usually around $3, but can be as high as $10, depending on what is on offer.

WORD OF MOUTH. "[At the Bon Bini Festival, t]hey had a small amount of Aruban food that you can buy at stalls like you would see at a fair. An emcee introduced each of the groups of performers. They had a band of elderly men who played local music on bongo-type drums. A popular comedian on the island performed as the highlight act as a singer. They also had both adult and children female dancers doing traditional island dances." —travelenthusiast

Casinos

WORD OF MOUTH

"To us, Aruba is like Las Vegas with a beach, and we love that type of atmosphere."

—KVR

AMONG THE BIGGEST DRAWS IN ARUBA are the island's elaborate, pulsating casinos. Aruba offers up gambling venues closer in spirit and form to Las Vegas than any other island in the Caribbean. Perhaps it's the predominately American crowd, but the casinos remain busy and popular, and almost every big resort has one. Although people don't dress up as elegantly as they did in years gone by, most of the casinos still expect a somewhat more put-together look (in the evening, at least) than a T-shirt and flip-flops.

There was a time when women dressed in evening gowns and men donned suits for a chic, glamorous night in Aruba's casinos. In the mid-'80s, however, the Alhambra Casino opened, touting its philosophy of "barefoot elegance." Suddenly shorts and T-shirts became acceptable attire. The relaxed dress code made gaming seem an affordable pastime rather than a luxury.

Aruba's casinos now attract high rollers, low-stakes bettors, and nongamblers alike. Games include slot machines, blackjack (both beloved by North Americans), baccarat (preferred by South Americans), craps, roulette—even betting on sports events. Theaters, restaurants, bars, and cigar shops have added another dimension to the casinos. Now you can go out for dinner, take in a show, sip after-dinner drinks, and play blackjack all under one roof. In between games you can get to know other patrons and swap tips and tales. The many local entertainers who rotate among the casinos add to the excitement.

A SHORT GAMBLING PRIMER

For a short-form handbook on the rules, the odds, and the strategies for the most popular casino games—or for help deciding on the kind of action that suits your style— read on.

THE GOOD BETS

The first part of any viable casino strategy is to risk the most money on wagers that present the lowest edge for the house. Blackjack, craps, video poker, and baccarat are the most advantageous to the bettor in this regard. The two types of bets at baccarat have a house advantage of a little more than 1%. The basic line bets at craps, if backed up with full odds, can be as low as ½%. Blackjack and video poker, at times, can not only put you even with the house (a true 50–50 proposition), but actually give you a slight long-term advantage.

The Casablanca Casino in the Westin Aruba.

How can a casino possibly provide you with a 50–50 or even a positive expectation at some of its games? First, because a vast number of suckers make the bad bets (those with a house advantage of 5%–35%, such as roulette, keno, and slots) day in and day out. Second, because the casino knows that very few people are aware of the opportunities to beat the odds. Third, because it takes skill—requiring study and practice—to be in a position to exploit these opportunities the casino presents. However, a mere hour or two spent learning strategies for the beatable games will put you light years ahead of the vast majority of visitors who give the gambling industry an average 12% to 15% profit margin.

BACCARAT

The most "glamorous" game in the casino, baccarat is a version of *chemin de fer,* which is popular in European gambling halls. It's a favorite with high rollers because thousands of dollars are often staked on one hand. The Italian word *baccara* means "zero." This refers to the point value of 10s and picture cards. The game is run by four pit personnel. Two dealers sit side by side at the middle of the table. They handle the winning and losing bets and keep track of each player's "commission" (explained below). The caller stands in the middle of the other side of the table and dictates the action. The "ladderman" supervises the game and acts as final judge if any disputes arise.

HOW TO PLAY

Baccarat is played with eight decks of cards dealt from a large "shoe" (or cardholder). Each player is offered a turn at handling the shoe and dealing the cards. Two two-card hands are dealt facedown: the "player" and the "bank" hands. The player who deals the cards is called the banker, although the house banks both hands. The players bet on which hand—player or banker—will come closest to adding up to 9 (a "natural"). Ace through 9 retain face value, and 10s and picture cards are worth zero. If you have a hand adding up to more than 10, the number 10 is subtracted from the total. For example, if one hand contains a 10 and a 4, the hand adds up to 4. If the other holds an ace and a 6, it adds up to 7. If a hand has a 7 and a 9, it adds up to 6.

Depending on the two hands, the caller either declares a winner and loser (if either hand actually adds up to 8 or 9) or calls for another card for the player hand (if it totals 1, 2, 3, 4, 5, or 10). The bank hand then either stands pat or draws a card, determined by a complex series of rules depending on what the player's total is and dictated by the caller. When one or the other hand is declared a winner, the dealers go into action to pay off the winning wagers, collect the losing wagers, and add up the commission (usually 5%) that the house collects on the bank hand. Both bets have a house advantage of slightly more than 1%.

The player-dealer (or banker) holds the shoe as long as the bank hand wins. When the player hand wins, the shoe moves counterclockwise around the table. Players can refuse the shoe and pass it to the next player. Because the caller dictates the action, player responsibilities are minimal. It's not necessary to know the card-drawing rules, even if you're the banker.

BACCARAT STRATEGY

To bet, you only have to place your money in the bank, player, or tie box on the layout, which appears directly in front of where you sit. If you're betting that the bank hand will win, you put your chips in the bank box; bets for the player hand go in the player box. (Only real suckers bet on the tie.) Most players bet on the bank hand when they deal, since they "represent" the bank and to do otherwise would seem as if they were betting "against" themselves. This isn't really true, but it seems that way. Playing baccarat is a simple matter of guessing whether the player or banker hand will come closest to 9 and deciding how much to bet on the outcome.

BLACKJACK

HOW TO PLAY

You play blackjack against a dealer, and whichever of you comes closest to a card total of 21 wins. Number cards are worth their face value, picture cards are worth 10, and aces are worth either 1 or 11. (Hands with aces are known as "soft" hands. Always count the ace first as an 11. If you also have a 10, your total will be 21, not 11.) If the dealer has a 17 and you have a 16, you lose. If you have an 18 against a dealer's 17, you win (even money). If both you and the dealer have a 17, it's a tie (or "push") and no money changes hands. If you go over a total of 21 (or "bust"), you lose, even if the dealer also busts later in the hand. If your first two cards add up to 21 (a "natural"), you're paid 3 to 2. However, if the dealer also has a natural, it's a push. A natural beats a total of 21 achieved with more than two cards.

You're dealt two cards, either facedown or faceup, depending on the custom of the casino. The dealer also gives herself two cards, one facedown and one faceup (except in double-exposure blackjack, where both the dealer's cards are visible). Depending on your first two cards and the dealer's up card, you can **stand,** or refuse to take another card. You can **hit,** or take as many cards as you need until you stand or bust. You can **double down,** or double your bet and take one card. You can **split** a like pair; if you're dealt two 8s, for example, you can double your bet and play the 8s as if they're two hands. You can **buy insurance** if the dealer is showing an ace. Here you're wagering half your initial bet that the dealer *does* have a natural. If so, you lose your initial bet but are paid 2 to 1 on the insurance (which means the whole thing is a push). You can **surrender** half your initial bet if you're holding a bad hand (known as a "stiff") such as a 15 or 16 against a high-up card such as a 9 or 10.

BLACKJACK STRATEGY

Many people devote a great deal of time to learning complicated statistical schemes. However, if you don't have the time, energy, or inclination to get that seriously involved, the following basic strategies should allow you to play the game with a modicum of skill and a paucity of humiliation:

When your hand is a stiff (a total of 12, 13, 14, 15, or 16) and the dealer shows a 2, 3, 4, 5, or 6, always stand.

When your hand is a stiff and the dealer shows a 7, 8, 9, 10, or ace, always hit.

When you hold 17, 18, 19, or 20, always stand.

When you hold a 10 or 11 and the dealer shows a 2, 3, 4, 5, 6, 7, 8, or 9, always double down.

When you hold a pair of aces or a pair of 8s, always split.

Never buy insurance.

CRAPS

Craps is a dice game played at a large rectangular table with rounded corners. Up to 12 players can stand around the table. The layout is mounted at the bottom of a surrounding rail, which prevents the dice from being thrown off the table and provides an opposite wall against which to bounce the dice. It can require up to four pit personnel to run an action-packed, fast-paced game of craps. Two dealers handle the bets made on either side of the layout. A "stickman" wields the long wooden stick, curved at one end, which is used to move the dice around the table. The stickman also calls the number that's rolled and books the proposition bets made in the middle of the layout. The "boxman" sits between the two dealers, overseeing the game and settling any disputes.

HOW TO PLAY

Stand at the table wherever you can find an open space. You can start betting casino chips immediately, but you have to wait your turn to be the shooter. The dice are passed clockwise around the table (the stickman will give you the dice at the appropriate time). It's important, when you're the shooter, to roll the dice hard enough so they bounce off the end wall of the table. This shows that you're not trying to control the dice with a "soft roll."

CRAPS STRATEGY

Playing craps is fairly straightforward; it's the betting that's complicated. The basic concepts are as follows: If the first time the shooter rolls the dice he or she turns up a 7 or 11, that's called a "natural"—an automatic win. If a 2, 3, or 12 comes up on the first throw (called the "come-out roll"), that's termed "craps"—an automatic lose. Each of the numbers 4, 5, 6, 8, 9, or 10 on a first roll is known as a "point": the shooter keeps rolling the dice until the point comes up again. If a 7 turns up before the point does, that's another loser. When either the point or a losing 7 is rolled, this is known as a "decision," which happens on average every 3.3 rolls.

But "winning" and "losing" rolls of the dice are entirely relative in this game, because there are two ways you can bet at craps: "for" the shooter or "against" the shooter. Betting for means that the shooter will "make his point" (win). Betting against means that the shooter will "seven out" (lose). Either way, you're actually betting against the house, which books all wagers. If you're betting "for" on the come-out, you place your chips on the layout's "pass line." If a 7 or 11 is rolled, you win even money. If a 2, 3, or 12 (craps) is rolled, you lose your bet. If you're betting "against" on the come-out, you place your chips in the "don't pass bar." A 7 or 11 loses; a 2, 3, or 12 wins. A shooter can bet for or against himself, or against other players.

There are also roughly two-dozen wagers you can make on any single specific roll of the dice. Craps strategy books can give you the details on come/don't come, odds, place, buy, big six, field, and proposition bets.

ROULETTE

Roulette is a casino game that uses a perfectly balanced wheel with 38 numbers (0, 00, and 1 through 36), a small white ball, a large layout with 11 different betting options, and special "wheel chips." The layout organizes 11 different bets into 6 "inside bets" (the single numbers, or those closest to the dealer) and 5 "outside bets" (the grouped bets, or those closest to the players).

The dealer spins the wheel clockwise and the ball counterclockwise. When the ball slows, the dealer announces, "No more bets." The ball drops from the "back track" to the "bottom track," caroming off built-in brass barriers and bouncing in and out of the different cups in the wheel before settling into the cup of the winning number. Then the dealer places a marker on the number and scoops all the losing chips into her corner. Depending on how crowded the game is, the casino can count on roughly 50 spins of the wheel per hour.

DID YOU KNOW?

Aruba offers the closest thing in the Caribbean to Las Vegas-style casino action, with some casinos in large hotels open 24 hours a day; the legal age for gambling is 18.

HOW TO PLAY

To buy in, place your cash on the layout near the wheel. Inform the dealer of the denomination of the individual unit you intend to play. Know the table limits (displayed on a sign in the dealer area). Don't ask for a 25¢ denomination if the minimum is $1. The dealer gives you a stack of wheel chips of a color that is different from those of all the other players and places a chip marker atop one of your wheel chips on the rim of the wheel to identify its denomination. Note that you must cash in your wheel chips at the roulette table before you leave the game. Only the dealer can verify how much they're worth.

ROULETTE STRATEGY

With **inside bets**, you can lay any number of chips (depending on the table limits) on a single number, 1 through 36 or 0 or 00. If the number hits, your payoff is 35 to 1, for a return of $36. You could, conceivably, place a $1 chip on all 38 numbers, but the return of $36 would leave you $2 short, which divides out to 5.26%, the house advantage. If you place a chip on the line between two numbers and one of those numbers hits, you're paid 17 to 1 for a return of $18 (again, $2 short of the true odds). Betting on three numbers returns 11 to 1, four numbers returns 8 to 1, five numbers pays 6 to 1 (this is the worst bet at roulette, with a 7.89% disadvantage), and six numbers pays 5 to 1.

To place an **outside bet**, lay a chip on one of three "columns" at the lower end of the layout next to numbers 34, 35, and 36. This pays 2 to 1. A bet placed in the first 12, second 12, or third 12 boxes also pays 2 to 1. A bet on red or black, odd or even, and 1 through 18 or 19 through 36 pays off at even money, 1 to 1. If you think you can bet on red *and* black, or odd *and* even, in order to play roulette and drink for free all night, think again. The green 0 or 00, which fall outside these two basic categories, will come up on average once every 19 spins of the wheel.

SLOT MACHINES

Around the turn of 20th century, Charlie Fey built the first slot in his San Francisco basement. Today hundreds of models accept everything from pennies to specially minted $500 tokens. The major advance in the game is the progressive jackpot. Banks of slots within a casino are connected by computer, and the jackpot total is displayed on a digital meter above the machines. Generally, the total increases by 5% of the wager. If you're playing a dollar machine,

6

Craps at the Crystal Casino in the Renaissance Aruba.

each time you pull the handle (or press the spin button), a nickel is added to the jackpot.

HOW TO PLAY

To play, insert your penny, nickel, quarter, silver dollar, or dollar token into the slot at the far right edge of the machine. Pull the handle or press the spin button, and then wait for the reels to spin and stop one by one, and for the machine to determine whether you're a winner (occasionally) or a loser (the rest of the time). It's pretty simple, but because there are so many types of machines nowadays, be sure you know exactly how the one you're playing operates.

SLOT-MACHINE STRATEGY

The house advantage on slots varies from machine to machine, between 3% and 25%. Casinos that advertise a 97% payback are telling you that at least one of their slot machines has a house advantage of 3%. Which one? There's really no way of knowing. Generally, $1 machines pay back at a higher percentage than quarter or nickel machines. On the other hand, machines with smaller jackpots pay back more money more frequently, meaning that you'll be playing with more of your winnings.

One of the all-time great myths about slot machines is that they're "due" for a jackpot. Slots, like roulette, craps, keno, and Big Six, are subject to the Law of Independent Trials, which means the odds are permanently and unalterably fixed. If the odds of lining up three sevens on a 25¢ slot machine have been set by the casino at 1 in 10,000, then those odds remain 1 in 10,000 whether the three 7s have been hit three times in a row or not hit for 90,000 plays. Don't waste a lot of time playing a machine that you suspect is "ready," and don't think if someone hits a jackpot on a particular machine only minutes after you've finished playing on it that it was "yours."

VIDEO POKER
This section deals only with straight-draw video poker.

Like blackjack, video poker is a game of strategy and skill, and at select times on select machines the player actually holds the advantage, however slight, over the house. Unlike with slot machines, you can determine the exact edge of video-poker machines. Like slots, however, video-poker machines are often tied into a progressive meter; when the jackpot total reaches high enough, you can beat the casino at its own game. The variety of video-poker machines is growing steadily. All are played in similar fashion, but the strategies are different.

HOW TO PLAY
The schedule for the payback on winning hands is posted on the machine, usually above the screen. It lists the returns for a high pair (generally jacks or better), two pair, three of a kind, a flush, full house, straight flush, four of a kind, and royal flush, depending on the number of coins played—usually 1, 2, 3, 4, or 5. Look for machines that pay with a single coin played: 1 coin for "jacks or better" (meaning a pair of jacks, queens, kings, or aces; any other pair is a stiff), 2 coins for two pairs, 3 for three of a kind, 6 for a flush, 9 for a full house, 50 for a straight flush, 100 for four of a kind, and 250 for a royal flush. This is known as a 9/6 machine—one that gives a nine-coin payback for a full house and a six-coin payback for a flush with one coin played. Other machines are known as 8/5 (eight for a full house, five for a flush), 7/5, and 6/5.

You want a 9/6 machine because it gives you the best odds: the return from a standard 9/6 straight-draw machine is 99.5%; you give up only half a percent to the house. An 8/5 machine returns 97.3%. On 6/5 machines, the figure drops to 95.1%, slightly less than roulette. Machines with varying paybacks are scattered throughout the casinos. In

The Copacabana Casino at the Hyatt-Regency Aruba.

some you'll see an 8/5 machine right next to a 9/6, and someone will be blithely playing the 8/5 machine.

As with slot machines, it's optimum to play the maximum number of coins to qualify for the jackpot. You insert five coins into the slot and press the "deal" button. Five cards appear on the screen—say, 5, jack, queen, 5, 9. To hold the pair of 5s, you press the hold buttons under the first and fourth cards. The word "hold" appears underneath the two 5s. You then press the "draw" button (often the same button as "deal") and three new cards appear on the screen—say, 10, jack, 5. You have three 5s. With five coins bet, the machine will give you 15 credits. Now you can press the "max bet" button: five units will be removed from your credits, and five new cards will appear on the screen. You repeat the hold and draw process; if you hit a winning hand, the proper payback will be added to your credits. Those who want coins rather than credit can hit the "cash out" button at any time. Some machines don't have credit counters and automatically dispense coins for a winning hand.

VIDEO-POKER STRATEGY
Like blackjack, video poker has a basic strategy that's been formulated by the computer simulation of hundreds of millions of hands. The most effective way to learn it is with a video poker–computer program that deals the cards on your screen, then tutors you in how to play each hand

Good-Luck Charms

Arubans take myths and superstitions very seriously. They flinch if a black butterfly flits into their home, because this symbolizes death. They gasp if a child crawls under their legs, because it's a sign that the baby won't grow anymore. And on New Year's Eve they toss the first sips of whiskey, rum, or champagne from the first bottle that's opened in the New Year out the door of their house to show respect to those who have died and to wish luck on others. It's no surprise, then, that good-luck charms are part of Aruba's casino culture as well.

The island's most common good-luck charm is the *djucu* (pronounced *joo*-koo), a brown-and-black stone that comes from the sea and becomes hot when rubbed. Many people have them put in gold settings—with their initials engraved in the metal—and wear them around their necks on a chain with other charms such as an anchor or a cross. Another item that's thought to bring good luck is a small bag of sand. Women wear them tucked discreetly into their bras; one woman who visited Aruba every year always carried a few cloves of garlic in her bag. On a recent visit, she removed the garlic, placed it on a slot machine, and won $1,000 instantly. All the more reason to save the scraps from your salad plate when you leave dinner.

6

---

properly. If you don't want to devote that much time to the study of video poker, memorizing these six rules will help you make the right decision for more than half the hands you'll be dealt:

If you're dealt a completely "stiff" hand (no like cards and no picture cards), draw five new cards.

If you're dealt a hand with no like cards but with one jack, queen, king, or ace, always hold on to the picture card; if you're dealt two different picture cards, hold both. But if you're dealt three different picture cards, hold only two (the two of the same suit, if that's an option).

If you're dealt a pair, hold it, no matter the face value.

Never hold a picture card with a pair of 2s through 10s.

Never draw two cards to try for a straight or a flush.

Never draw one card to try for an inside straight.

The Renaissance Aruba's private island.

THE CASINOS

Except for the free-standing Alhambra, most casinos are found in hotels; all are along Palm Beach or Eagle Beach or in downtown Oranjestad. Although the minimum age to enter is 18, some venues are relaxed about this rule. By day "barefoot elegance" is the norm in all casinos, although many establishments have a shirt-and-shoes requirement. Evening dress is expected to be more polished, though still casual. In high season the casinos are open from just before noon to the wee hours; in low season (May to November) they may not start dealing until late afternoon.

If you plan to play large sums of money, check in with the casino upon arrival so that you can be rewarded for your business. Most hotels offer gambling goodies—complimentary meals at local restaurants, chauffeured tours, and, in the cases of big spenders, high-roller suites. Even small-scale gamblers may be entitled to coupons for meals and discounted rooms.

★ In the casual **Alhambra Casino** (⊠*L. G. Smith Blvd. 47, Oranjestad* ☎*297/583–5000 Ext. 480 or 482*), amid the Spanish-style arches and leaded glass, a "Moorish slave" named Roger gives every gambler a hearty handshake upon entering. The atmosphere is casual, and with $5 tables, no one need feel intimidated. Try your luck at blackjack, Caribbean stud poker, three-card poker, roulette, craps, or one of the 300 slot machines that accept American nickels, quarters, and dollars. Head to one of the novelty touch-screen machines, each of which has a variety of games. There's also bingo every Saturday, Monday, and Thursday beginning at 1 PM. If you fill your card, you can collect the grand prize of a few hundred dollars—not bad for a $5 investment. Be sure to sign up for the Alhambra Advantage Card, which gives you a point for each dollar you spend—even if you lose at the tables, you can still go home with prizes. Of course, winners can spend their earnings immediately at the many on-site shops. The casino is owned by the Divi Divi resorts, and golf carts run to and from nearby hotels every 15 minutes or so. The slots here open daily at 10 AM; gaming tables operate from 6 PM until 4 AM.

The **Aruban Casino** (⊠ *J. E. Irausquin Blvd. 250, Eagle Beach* ☎ *877/298–5167* ⊕ *www.thearuban.com*), formerly the Royal Cabana, has been completely redone with an elegant new look and the latest in gaming equipment. This is reputed to be one of the largest casinos in the Caribbean, and it looks it. Those not interested in gambling can enjoy live entertainment and a choice of two restaurants.

The **Casablanca Casino** (⊠ *Westin Aruba Resort, Spa & Casino, J. E. Irausquin Blvd. 77, Palm Beach* ☎ *297/586–4466*) is the Westin Aruba Beach Resort & Casino's quietly elegant casino, which has a Humphrey Bogart theme and a tropical color scheme. Spend some time at the blackjack, roulette, craps, stud poker, and baccarat tables, or the slot machines. Seek out the unique Feature Frenzy machines, which reportedly pay out $6,000 jackpots daily. If gambling isn't your style, visit the Casablanca Casino Bar for exotic cocktails and live jazz most nights at 9. Or you can take in the Aruba Carnival Havana Tropical shows. The casino is open daily from noon to 4 AM.

The **Casino at the Radisson Aruba Resort** (⊠ *Radisson Aruba Resort & Casino, J. E. Irausquin Blvd. 81, Palm Beach* ☎ *297/586–4045*) may be hard to find, even though it measures 16,000 square feet. Descend the stairs at the corner of the resort's lobby, following the sounds of the piano player's tunes. The nightly action here includes Las Vegas–style blackjack, roulette, craps, and slot machines. Overhead, thousands of lights simulate shooting stars that seem destined to carry out your wishes for riches. A host of shops and restaurants let you chip away at your new-found wealth. The slots here open daily at noon, and the table action begins at 6 PM. Everything shuts down at 4 AM.

★ Ablaze with neon, the Hyatt Regency Aruba Beach Resort's ultramodern **Copacabana Casino** (⊠*Hyatt Regency Aruba Beach Resort & Casino, J. E. Irausquin Blvd. 85, Palm Beach* ☎297/586–1234) is an enormous complex with a Carnival-in-Rio theme. The most popular games here are slots, blackjack, craps, and baccarat. Slots and some other games are available at noon, the dice start rolling at 6 PM, and all other pursuits are open by 8 PM. From 9 PM to 2 AM there's live music at the stage near the bar—you'll find it hard to steal away from the pulsating mix of Latin and American tunes. Don't forget to register for free dinners and brunches and hotel discounts at the hostess station. The casino is open until 4 AM.

★ Adorned with Austrian crystal chandeliers and gold-leaf columns, the Renaissance Aruba Beach Resort Marina Tower's glittering **Crystal Casino** (⊠*Renaissance Aruba Resort & Casino, L. G. Smith Blvd. 82, Oranjestad* ☎297/583–6000) evokes Monaco's grand establishments—hence, the international clientele. The Salon Privé offers serious gamblers a private room for baccarat, roulette, and high-stakes blackjack. This casino is popular among cruise-ship passengers, who stroll over from the port to watch and play in slot tournaments and bet on sporting events. The Crystal Lounge, which overlooks the betting floor, serves up live music along with the cocktails, and the Crystal Theater's shows—*Let's Go Latin* and *Aruba Panorama*—are big hits on the island.

The Holiday Inn SunSpree Aruba Beach Resort's **Excelsior Casino** (⊠*Holiday Inn SunSpree Aruba Beach Resort & Casino, J. E. Irausquin Blvd. 230, Palm Beach* ☎297/586–3600)—the birthplace of Caribbean stud poker—has blackjack, craps, and roulette tables, plenty of slot machines, and a bar featuring live entertainment. There's also a poker room for Texas hold 'em, seven-card stud, and Caribbean stud. It's the only casino on Palm Beach with an ATM adjacent to the cashier. Afternoon bingo overtakes the main floor every weekday at 3:30 PM. The casino is open daily from 8 AM to 4 AM; slots begin spinning at 9 AM, and tables open at 12:30 PM.

The **Royal Palm Casino** (⊠*J. E. Irausquin Blvd. 83, Palm Beach* ☎297/586–9039 ⊕*www.occidentalhotels.com/ grand*) at the Occidental Grand Resort opens daily at noon

The Seaport Casino is the only Aruba casino actually on the waterfront.

for slots and at 5 PM for all other games. Famous movie stars gaze down at you from a 30-foot mural as you take your chances at one of 245 slots or at dozens of blackjack, roulette, poker, craps, baccarat, and Caribbean stud poker tables. The entire gaming floor joins in the free full-card bingo game held nightly at 10:30. Anyone who scores a full card within the first 50 calls wins a clean grand; everyone who shows a full card after that walks away with $100. There's a slot tournament every Friday at 8 PM, and look for double jackpots daily from 3 to 5 PM. The nightly bingo game always draws a crowd with a jackpot of $2,000. You can hang around until 4 AM.

The **Riu Palace Casino** (⊠ *J. E. Irausquin Blvd. 79, Palm Beach* ☎ *297/586–3900*) leans toward opulence, with a preponderance of dark woods and lavish fabrics. Though not the largest on the island, it offers a range of activities including blackjack and baccarat tables, slots, roulette and cocktails galore.

Seaport Casino (⊠ *L. G. Smith Blvd. 9, Oranjestad* ☎ *297/583– 6000*) offers low-key gambling at a waterside location adjacent to the Renaissance Aruba Beach Resort's Beach Tower, the Renaissance Marketplace, and the Renaissance Conference Center. More than 200 slot machines are in daily operation from 10 AM to 4 AM, and tables are open from 4 PM to 4 AM. From here you can see the boats on the ocean and enjoy not only the games you'd find at other casinos but also shops, restaurants, bars, and movie theaters. Stop by on Tuesday, Thursday, or Sunday for the casino's popular bingo tournaments.

★ The Aruba Marriott Resort's **Stellaris Casino** (⊠ *Aruba Marriott Resort, L. G. Smith Blvd. 101, Palm Beach* ☎ *297/586–9000*) has mirrors on the ceilings that reflect the glamorous chandeliers. This 24-hour facility is sure to be able to keep early-morning or late-night gamblers happy. Take your pick of craps, roulette, Caribbean stud poker, minibaccarat, and superbuck (like blackjack with suits). Every night except Sunday there's a performance by musician Cesar Olarta that may boost your luck. Check in with the casino when you arrive at the hotel and you can get a membership card. If you play high enough stakes at the tables, you can win free meals and other prizes. If not, you can at least get a postcard in the mail offering a special rate on future stays. The hotel offers a 30% discount to those who play at least four hours each day.

Sports and Activities

WORD OF MOUTH

"There are plenty of things to do: snorkeling, wind-surfing, diving, fishing, and lots of 'things that go fast in the water' for you to drive."

—Auntie-Mame

ABOVE THE SURFACE AND BELOW, Aruban waters are brimming with activity. Although beach bumming is a popular pastime, golf, tennis, and horseback riding are also good options. More adventurous souls can explore the terrain on a motorcycle, parasail through the Aruban sky, or harness the power of the wind on a kiteboard. Constant trade winds have made Aruba an internationally recognized windsurfing destination. The crystalline waters of the island's leeward side offer scuba divers and snorkelers a kaleidoscopic adventure day or night.

BEACHES

The beaches on Aruba are legendary: white sand, turquoise waters, and virtually no litter—everyone takes the NO TIRA SUSHI (no littering) signs very seriously, especially considering the island's $280 fine. The major public beaches, which back up to the hotels along the southwestern strip, are usually crowded. You can make the hour-long hike from the Holiday Inn to the Tamarijn without ever leaving sand. Make sure you're well protected from the sun—it scorches fast despite the cooling trade winds. Luckily, there's at least one covered bar (and often an ice-cream stand) at virtually every hotel. On the island's northeastern side stronger winds make the waters too choppy for swimming, but the vistas are great and the terrain is wonderful for exploring.

Arashi Beach. Just after Malmok Beach, this is a 0.5-mi (1-km) stretch of gleaming white sand. Although it was once rocky, nature—with a little help from humans—has turned it into an excellent place for sunbathing and swimming. Despite calm waters, the rocky reputation has kept most people away, making it relatively uncrowded. ⊠ *West of Malmok Beach, on west end.*

☾ **Baby Beach.** On the island's eastern tip (near the refinery),
★ this semicircular beach borders a placid bay that's just about as shallow as a wading pool—perfect for tots, shore divers, and terrible swimmers. Thatched shaded areas are good places to cool off. Down the road is the island's rather unusual pet cemetery. Stop by the nearby snack truck for burgers, hot dogs, beer, and soda. The road to this beach (and several others) is through San Nicolas and along the road toward Seroe Colorado. Just before reaching the beach, keep an eye out for a strange 300-foot natural seawall made of coral and rock that was thrown up overnight

Sidney Ponson: Pitcher

When he was growing up in Aruba, Sidney Ponson loved sailing, scuba diving, and just about anything to do with the ocean. "My life was the beach," says Ponson, "before baseball." He started playing baseball when he was nine, even though the game was pretty difficult on an arid island where the fields are full of rocks. But employment on his uncle's boat taught him to work hard for what he wanted in life.

The pitcher signed with the minor leagues at 16, then was tapped by the Baltimore Orioles by the time he was 21. Hitting the big leagues involved lots of hard work (his grueling workouts last from 7:30 AM to 1 PM and involve lifting weights, running, and throwing), but Ponson says it was worth it when he got the call to play. "It was 6:30 AM, and I was on a road trip in a hotel in Scranton," he remembers. "They told me when to show up and said to be ready to play at 8:30."

Now, Ponson spends 10 months a year in the United States pitching for his current team, the St. Louis Cardinals, and two months in Aruba resting and visiting family and friends. Ponson uses his status as a major leaguer to do some good for his island. He and fellow Aruban baseball player Calvin Maduro draft other professional baseball players, including Pedro Martinez and Manny Ramirez, to play in an annual celebrity softball game to raise funds for Aruba's Cas pa Hubentud, a home for underprivileged children.

To prepare for a game, Ponson heads to the clubhouse for some serious stretching to the hard-rock music of Metallica, AC/DC, or Mötley Crüe. How does it feel right before he heads out to pitch? "One million people want to do what I do—play ball in front of 50,000 people every night," says Ponson, "and that's a great feeling."

7

when Hurricane Ivan swept by the island in 2004. ⊠*Near Seroe Colorado, on east end.*

Boca Catalina. Although there are some stones and pebbles along this white-sand beach, snorkelers come for the shallow water filled with fish. Swimmers will also appreciate the calm conditions. There aren't any facilities nearby, however, so pack provisions. ⊠ *Between Arashi Beach and Malmok Beach, north of intersection of 1B and 2B.*

Boca Grandi. This is a great spot for windsurfers, but swimming is not advisable. It's near Seagrape Grove and the

Aruba Golf Club toward the island's eastern tip. ⊠*Near Seagrape Grove, on east end.*

Boca Prins. You'll need a four-wheel-drive vehicle to make the trek to this strip of coastline, which is famous for its backdrop of enormous vanilla sand dunes. Near the Fontein Cave and Blue Lagoon, the beach itself is about as large as a Brazilian bikini—but with two rocky cliffs and tumultuously crashing waves, it's as romantic as Aruba gets. This isn't a swimming beach, however. Bring a picnic, a beach blanket, and sturdy sneakers, and descend the rocks that form steps to the water's edge. ⊠*Off 7 A/B, near Fontein Cave.*

Boca Tabla. This east-side beach, also called Bachelor's Beach, is known for its white-powder sand and good snorkeling and windsurfing. Don't head here for the swimming (conditions aren't the best) or the facilities (there aren't any). ⊠*East end, south of Boca Grandi.*

Dos Playa. Hire a four-wheel-drive vehicle, pack a blanket and a picnic basket, and head here to take in the beautiful view. Swimming is discouraged because of strong currents and massive waves. ⊠*Arikok National Park, just south of Boca Prins.*

Druif Beach. Fine white sand and calm water make this "tops-optional" beach a fine choice for sunbathing and swimming. Convenience is a highlight, too: the many Divi hotels are close at hand, and the beach is accessible by bus, rental car, or taxi. ⊠*Parallel to J.E. Irausquin Blvd., near Divi resorts, south of Punta Brabo.*

★ **Fodor's Choice Eagle Beach.** On the southwestern coast, across the highway from what is quickly becoming known as Time-Share Lane, is one of the Caribbean's—if not the world's—best beaches. Not long ago it was a nearly deserted stretch of pristine sand dotted with the occasional thatched picnic hut. Now that the resorts have been completed, this mile-plus-long beach is always hopping. When other Caribbean beaches eroded after Hurricane Ivan in 2004, Eagle Beach actually became several feet wider. ⊠*J. E. Irausquin Blvd., north of Manchebo Beach.*

Fisherman's Huts. Next to the Holiday Inn is a windsurfer's haven with good swimming conditions. Take a picnic lunch (tables are available) and watch the elegant purple, aqua, and orange sails struggle in the wind. ⊠*1 A/B, at Holiday Inn SunSpree Aruba.*

Grapefield Beach. To the southeast of San Nicolas, a sweep of blinding-white sand in the shadow of cliffs and boulders is marked by an anchor-shape memorial dedicated to all seamen. Pick sea grapes from January to June. Swim at your own risk; the waves here can be rough. ⊠*Southwest of San Nicolas, on east end.*

Malmok Beach. On the northwestern shore, this small, nondescript beach (where some of Aruba's wealthiest families have built tony residences) borders shallow waters that stretch 300 yards from shore. It's the perfect place to learn to windsurf. Right off the coast here is a favorite haunt for divers and snorkelers—the wreck of the German ship *Antilla*, scuttled in 1940. Take J.E. Irausquin Boulevard to the very end of the road. ⊠*At end of J.E. Irausquin Blvd., Malmokweg.*

Manchebo Beach *(Punta Brabo).* Impressively wide, the shoreline in front of the Manchebo Beach Resort is where officials turn a blind eye to the occasional topless sunbather. This beach merges with Druif Beach, and most locals use the name Manchebo to refer to both. ⊠*J.E. Irausquin Blvd., at Manchebo Beach Resort.*

WORD OF MOUTH. "The ocean [at Manchebo Beach] had a stretch of shells and rocks at the entrance to the beach due to the storm that happened the week before we arrived. After we got past the shells, the floor of the ocean was smooth and sandy." —travelenthusiast

Mangel Halto. Drive or cab it over to this east-side beach, also known as Savaneta. It's a lovely setting for a picnic. Hop into the shallow waters for a swim after taking in the sun on the fine white sand. ⊠*Between Savaneta and Pos Chiquito.*

WORD OF MOUTH. "For an out of the way beach with no facilities, try the Mangel Hato. You'll need a car to get there." —KVR

Palm Beach. This stretch runs from the Westin Aruba Resort, Spa & Casino to the Marriott Aruba Ocean Club. It's the center of Aruban tourism, offering good opportunities for swimming, sailing, and other water sports. In some spots you might find a variety of shells that are great to collect, but not as much fun to step on barefoot—bring sandals just in case. ⊠*J.E. Irausquin Blvd. between Westin Aruba Resort, Spa & Casino and Marriott Aruba Ocean Club.*

WORD OF MOUTH. "Palm Beach . . . is a beautiful beach for long walks and sunsets." —OceanBreeze1

☺ **Rodger's Beach.** Near Baby Beach on the island's eastern tip, this beautiful curving stretch of sand is only slightly marred by its proximity to the oil refinery at the bay's far side. Swimming conditions are excellent here, as demonstrated by the local kids diving off the piers. The snack bar at the water's edge has beach-equipment rentals and a shop. Local bands play Sunday nights from Easter through summer. Drive around the refinery perimeter to get here. ⊠*Next to Baby Beach, on east end.*

Santo Largo. Swimming conditions are good—thanks to shallow water edged by white-powder sand—but there are no facilities at this beach west of Mangel Halto. ⊠*Just west of Savaneta.*

Surfside. Accessible by public bus, car, or taxi, this beach is the perfect place to swim. It's also conveniently located next to the Havana Beach Club and across the street from the Caribbean Town Beach Resort. ⊠*Off L.G. Smith Blvd, Oranjestad, just before airport compound.*

ACTIVITIES

ADVENTURE GAMES

☺ Paintball aficionados can unite in a messier version of capture the flag. The game is played with air guns that propel biodegradable gelatin capsules that splatter you with water-soluble paint on impact. To win, simply return the opposing team's flag to your own team's station without being hit by a pellet. Games (complete with equipment and protective gear) are run by **Events in Motion** (⊠*Rancho Daimari, Tanki Leendert 249, Plantage Daimari* ☎297/587–5675 ⊕*www.visitaruba.com/ranchodaimari*). Games last about two hours, costing $40 per person with a minimum of 10 people. You must make reservations three days in advance.

BIKING AND MOTORCYCLING

Biking is a great way to get around the island; the climate is perfect, and the trade winds help keep you cool. If you prefer to exert less energy while reaping the rewards of the outdoors, a scooter is a great way to whiz from place to

Relatively flat, Aruba is the perfect biking destination.

place. Or let your hair down completely and cruise around on a Harley Davidson.

ORGANIZED EXCURSIONS

Aruba Off-Road (⊠ *Rancho Del Campo, Sombre 22E, Santa Cruz* ☎*297/595–0290* ⊕ *www.arubaoffroad.com*) offers an unbelievable experience as you drive through the country-side in a Tomcar four-wheeler. These odd-looking vehicles are like a cross between a dune buggy and a tank, and seem to be able to manage the most challenging terrain with no difficulty. The noise from the rear-mounted engine will leave you giddy, as will the experience of driving over boulders and up steep hills. The Baby Beach tour allows a good sampling of terrain and includes safety equipment, water, and snacks for $109 per person, with two people sharing the vehicle (you can bounce solo for $139). This is not an experience you are likely to forget, despite the fact it is actually very safe.

Big Twin Aruba (⊠*L.G. Smith Blvd. 124-A, Oranjestad* ☎*297/582–8660* ⊕*www.harleydavidson-aruba.com*) ful-fills every biker's fantasy. With an initial $1,000 deposit, rates are $163 for a day or $130 for a half-day (including insurance and helmets). The dealership also sells Harley clothing, accessories, and collectibles. Be sure to pose for a photo next to the classic 1939 Liberator on display in the showroom. The shop is open Monday through Saturday from 9 to 6.

If you prefer motoring with folks who are in the know, **De Palm Tours** (✉*L.G. Smith Blvd. 142, Oranjestad* ☎*297/582–4400 or 800/766–6016* ⊕*www.depalm.com*) offers four-to eight-hour guided tours on all-terrain vehicles that pass through Arikok National Park en route to Natural Bridge. Prices range from $75 to $190. De Palm also conducts a half-day four-wheel-drive tour called the Aruba Safari, one of the most popular trips on the island. The cost is $75. These trips give you plenty of time to swim, and sometimes include lunch.

Rancho Notorious (✉*Boroncana, Noord* ☎*297/586–0508* ⊕*www.ranchonotorious.com*) organizes mountain-biking tours and provides the bikes as well.

RENTALS

There are plenty of dealers around who will be happy to help you in your motoring pursuits.

Donata Car and Cycle (✉*L. G. Smith Blvd. 136-D, Oranjestad* ☎*297/587–8300*) rents motorcycles and mopeds.

For scooters and all-terrain vehicles, head to **George's Cycle Center** (✉*L. G. Smith Blvd. 136, Oranjestad* ☎*297/592–5875*).

Melchor Cycle Rental (✉*Bubali 106B, Noord* ☎*297/587–1787*) rents ATVs and bikes.

Semver Cycle Rental (✉*Noord 22, Noord* ☎*297/586–6851*) will help you choose the motorcycle or scooter that matches your experience level and your plans for the day.

Pablito's Bike & Locker Rental (✉*L.G. Smith Blvd. 234, Oranjestad* ☎*297/587–0047*) rents mountain bikes for $20 a day.

BOWLING

☯ The **Eagle Bowling Palace** (✉*Sasakiweg, Pos Abou, Oranjestad* ☎*297/583–5038*) has 16 lanes, a snack bar, and a cocktail lounge. It's open Monday and Tuesday from 5 PM to 1 AM; Sunday, Wednesday, and Thursday from 10 AM to 1 AM; and on Friday and Saturday from 10 AM to 2 AM. Children under 12 can bowl until 7 PM. One lane for one hour will cost $12 to $15, depending on the time of day.

DAY SAILS

If you plan to take a cruise around the island, know that the trade winds can make the waters choppy, and that catamaran rides are much smoother than those on single-hull boats. Sucking on a peppermint or ginger candy may soothe your queasy stomach; avoid boating with an empty or overly full stomach. Moonlight cruises cost about $45 per person. There are also a variety of snorkeling, dinner and dancing, and sunset party cruises to choose from, priced from $30 to $60 per person. Many of the smaller operators work out of their homes; they often offer to pick you up (and drop you off) at your hotel or meet you at a particular hotel pier.

De Palm Tours (⊠ *L.G. Smith Blvd. 142, Oranjestad* ☎ *297/582–4400 or 800/766–6016* ⊕ *www.depalm.com*) will sail you over the open seas for a two- to four-hour snorkeling adventure at nearby reefs. The cost for the catamaran trip is $49 per person.

Mi Dushi (⊠ *Turibana Plaza, Noord 124, Noord* ☎ *297/586–2010* ⊕ *www.midushi.com*), a ship whose name means "My Sweetheart," offers daytime snorkeling trips on this romantic two-masted ship include breakfast, lunch, and drinks for $59 per person. It also offers popular sunset happy-hour cruises (*see* ⇨ *Cruises in Chapter 5, Nightlife*).

★ **Octopus Sailing Charters** (⊠ *Sali-a Cerca 1G, Oranjestad* ☎ *297/586–4281* ⊕ *www.octopusaruba.com*) operates a trimaran that holds about 20 people. The drinks flow freely during the three-hour afternoon sail, which costs $33. Having a captain named Jethro is almost worth the price of admission in itself.

Pelican Tours & Watersports (⊠ *Pelican Pier, near Holiday Inn and Playa Linda hotels, Palm Beach* ☎ *297/586–3271* ⊕ *www.pelican-aruba.com*) offers daytime snorkeling trips to two different reefs for about $47 per person. The company also offers sunset sails for the same price that can be combined with dinner at the Pelican Restaurant on Palm Beach.

Red Sail Sports (⊠ *L.G. Smith Blvd. 17, Oranjestad* ☎ *297/583–1603, 877/733–7245 in U.S.* ⊕ *www.redsailaruba.com*) offers a number of packages aboard its four catamarans, including the 70-foot *Rumba*. The popular sunset sail includes drinks and a lively atmosphere for $45 per person; the dinner cruise package includes a three-course

Snorkeling from a replica pirate ship.

meal and open bar for $95. Red Sail Sports also has desks at the Hyatt and Occidental hotels.

The **Seaport Marina** (⊠*Seaport Marketplace 204, Oranjestad*) is the place to go for charters.

Tranquilo Charters Aruba (⊠*Sibelius St. 25, Oranjestad* ☎*297/586–1418* ⊕*www.visitaruba.com/tranquilo*), operated by Captain Hagedoorn, offers entertaining cruises, including a six-hour cruise to the south side of the island with lunch for $65. As strange as it sounds, the special "mom's Dutch pea soup" served with lunch is actually very good. Snorkeling equipment and free lessons are included in the package.

Wave Dancer Cruises (⊠*Ponton 90, Oranjestad* ☎*297/582–5520* ⊕*www.arubawavedancer.com*), in business since the mid-1970s, offers excellent value for the money. Sunset sails are $37, including drinks and snacks; half-day sails are $70, including snacks, lunch, and drinks. Snorkeling packages are also available.

FISHING

Deep-sea catches here include barracuda, kingfish, wahoo, bonito, and black-and-yellow tuna. November to April is the catch-and-release season for sailfish and marlin. Many skippered charter boats are available for half- or full-day sails. Packages include tackle, bait, and refreshments. Prices

"Go On with the Struggle"

Arubans are proud of their autonomous standing within the Kingdom of the Netherlands, and Gilberto François "Betico" Croes is heralded as the hero behind the island's *status aparte* (separate status). His birthday, January 25, is an official Aruban holiday.

During the Dutch colonial expansion of the 17th century, Aruba and five other islands—Bonaire, Curaçao, St. Maarten, St. Eustatius, and Saba—became territories known as the Netherlands Antilles. After World War II these islands began to pressure Holland for autonomy, and in 1954 they became a collective self-governing entity under the umbrella of the Kingdom of the Netherlands.

At that time, several political parties were in power on the island. Soon, however, Juancho Irausquin (who has a major thoroughfare named in his honor) formed a new party that maintained control for nearly two decades. Irausquin was considered the founder of Aruba's new economic order and the precursor of modern Aruban politics. After his death his party's power diminished.

In 1971 Croes, then a young, ambitious school administrator, became the leader of another political party. Bolstered by a thriving economy generated by Aruba's oil refinery, Croes spearheaded the island's cause to secede from the Netherlands Antilles and to gain status as an equal partner within the Dutch kingdom. Sadly, he didn't live to celebrate the realization of his dream. On December 31, 1985, the day before Aruba's new status became official, Croes was in a car accident that put him in a coma for 11 months. He died on November 26, 1986. Etched in the minds of Arubans are his prophetic words: *"Si mi cai na cominda, gara e bandera y sigui cu e lucha"* ("If I die along the way, seize the flag and go on with the struggle").

range from $250 to $450 for a half-day charter and from $400 to $700 for a full day.

Contact **De Palm Tours** (⊠*L. G. Smith Blvd. 142, Oranjestad* ☎*297/582–4400 or 800/766–6016* ⊕*www.depalm.com*) for a choice of fishing excursions.

Pelican Tours & Watersports (⊠*Pelican Pier, near Holiday Inn and Playa Linda hotels, Palm Beach* ☎*297/586–3271* ⊕*www.pelican-aruba.com*) is not just for the surf-and-snorkel crowd; the company will help you catch trophy-size fish.

Red Sail Sports (✉*J. E. Irausquin Blvd. 83, Oranjestad* ☎*297/586–1603, 877/733–7245 in U.S.* ⊕*www.redsail.com*) can arrange everything for your fishing trip.

Captain Kenny of **Teaser Charters** (✉*St. Vincentweg 5, Oranjestad* ☎*297/582–5088* ⊕*www.teasercharters.com*) runs a thrilling expedition. The expertise of the crew is matched by a commitment to sensible fishing practices, which include "catch and release" where appropriate and avoiding ecologically sensitive areas. The company's two boats are fully equipped, and the crews seem to have an uncanny ability to locate the best fishing spots.

GOLF

Golf may seem incongruous on an arid island such as Aruba, yet there are several popular courses. The constant trade winds and occasional stray goat add unexpected hazards.

�־ A moat surrounds the pair of elevated 18-hole miniature golf courses at **Adventure Golf & Fun Park** (✉*Joe Mendez Miniature Adventure Golf, Sasakiweg, Oranjestad* ☎*297/588–6576*). There are also paddleboats and bumper boats, a snack stand, and a bar. A round of 18 holes costs $7. It's open 5 PM to 1 AM during the week and from noon to 1 AM on the weekends.

The **Aruba Golf Club** (✉*Golfweg 82, San Nicolas* ☎*297/584–2006*) has a 9-hole course with 20 sand traps, five water traps, roaming goats, and lots of cacti. There are also 11 greens covered with artificial turf, making 18-hole tournaments a possibility. The clubhouse has a bar and locker rooms. Greens fees are $10 for 9 holes, $15 for 18 holes. Golf carts are available.

Aruba Golf & Leisure (✉*J.E. Irasquin Blvd. 326, Oranjestad* ☎*297/586–4590*) has a 300-yard driving range, an 18-hole putting green, and a chipping area. A bucket of balls will set you back $3, and you can rent a half set of clubs for $10. It's open from 7 AM to 11 PM daily.

The **Links at Divi Aruba** (✉*J.E. Irausquin Blvd. 93, Oranjestad* ☎*297/581–4653*) is a 9-hole course designed by Karl Litten and Lorie Viola. The par-36 paspalum grass course (best for seaside courses) takes you past beautiful lagoons. Ameni-

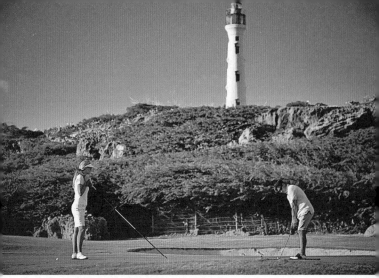

The California Lighthouse towers over Tierra del Sol golf course.

ties include a golf school with professional instruction, a swing analysis station, a driving range, and a two-story golf clubhouse with a pro shop. Two restaurants are available: Windows on Aruba for fine dining and Mulligan's for a casual and quick lunch. Greens fees are $85 for 9 holes, $124 for 18 from December to April; guests of the Divi properties pay a reduced rate.

★ **Tierra del Sol** (✉*Malmokweg* ☎*297/586–0978*), a stunning course, is on the northwest coast near the California Lighthouse. Designed by Robert Trent Jones Jr., this 18-hole championship course combines Aruba's native beauty— cacti and rock formations—with the lush greens of the world's best courses. The greens fee varies depending on the time of day (from December to March it is $158 in the morning, $124 for early afternoon and $100 from 3 PM) and includes a golf cart equipped with a communications system that allows you to order drinks for your return to the clubhouse. Half-day golf clinics, a bargain at $45, include lunch in the clubhouse (available Monday, Tuesday, and Thursday). The pro shop is one of the Caribbean's most elegant, with an extremely attentive staff.

Wildlife Watching

Wildlife abounds on Aruba. Look for the cottontail rabbit: the black patch on its neck likens it to a species found in Venezuela, spawning a theory that it was brought to the island by pre-Columbian peoples. Wild donkeys, originally transported to the island by the Spanish, are found in the more rugged terrain; sheep and goats roam freely throughout the island.

About 170 bird species make their home on Aruba year-round, and migratory birds temporarily raise the total to 300 species when they fly by in November and January. Among the highlights are the *trupiaal* (bright orange), the *prikichi* (a parakeet with a green body and yellow head), and the *barika geel* (a small, yellow-bellied bird with a sweet tooth—you may find one eating the sugar off your breakfast table). At Bubali Bird Sanctuary on the island's western side, you can see various types of waterfowl, especially cormorants, herons, scarlet ibis, and fish eagles. Along the south shore, brown pelicans are common. At Tierra

del Sol Golf Course in the north you may glimpse the *shoko*, the endangered burrowing owl.

Lizard varieties include large iguanas, once hunted for use in local soups and stews. (That practice is now illegal.) Like chameleons, these iguanas change color to adapt to their surroundings—from bright green when foraging in the foliage (which they love to eat) to a brownish shade when sunning themselves in the dirt. The *pega pega*—a cousin of the gecko—is named for the suction pads on its feet that allow it to grip virtually any surface (*pega* means "to stick" in Papiamento). The *kododo blauw* (whiptail lizard) is one of the species that is unique to the island.

Two types of snakes are found only on Aruba. The cat-eyed *santanero* isn't venomous, but it won't hesitate to defecate in your hand should you pick it up. The poisonous *cascabel* is a unique subspecies of rattlesnake that doesn't use its rattle. These snakes live in the area between Mount Yamanota, Fontein, and San Nicolas.

HIKING

Despite Aruba's arid landscape, hiking the rugged countryside will give you the best opportunities to see the island's wildlife and flora. Arikok National Wildlife Park is an excellent place to glimpse the real Aruba, free of the trappings of tourism. The heat can be oppressive, so be sure to take it easy, wear a hat, and have a bottle of water handy.

There are more than 34 km (20 mi) of trails in **Arikok National Park** (☎297/582–8001), concentrated in the island's eastern interior and along its northeastern coast. The park is crowned by Aruba's second-highest mountain, the 577-foot Mount Arikok, so climbing is also a possibility.

Hiking in the park, whether alone or in a group led by guides, is generally not too strenuous. Look for different colors to determine the degree of difficulty of each trail. Sturdy shoes are a must to grip the granular surfaces and climb the occasionally steep terrain. You should also exercise caution with the strong sun—bring along plenty of water and wear sunscreen and a hat. On the rare occasion that it rains, the park should be avoided completely, as mud makes both driving and hiking treacherous.

The Aruban government is working on a 10-year ecotourism plan to preserve the resources of the park, which makes up 18% of the island's total area. The effort includes setting aside areas for recreation, establishing zones where the natural habitats are protected, and developing a scenic loop roadway. At the park's main entrance, the Arikok Center houses offices, restrooms, and food facilities. Under the plan, all visitors stop here upon entering so that officials can manage the traffic flow and distribute information on park rules and features.

☼ ★ **Aruba Nature Sensitive Hikers** (✉*Pos Chiquito 13E, Savaneta* ☎*297/587–5017* ⊕*www.sensitivehikers.com*) is run by Eddy Croes, a former park ranger whose passion for the area is seemingly unbounded. Groups are never larger than eight people, so you'll see as much detail as you can handle. Expect frequent stops when Eddy will ask for silence so that you can hear the sounds of the park. The hikes are done at an easy pace and are suitable for basically anyone. A moonlight walk is available for those looking to avoid the heat.

HORSEBACK RIDING

Ranches offer short jaunts along the beach or longer rides along trails passing through countryside flanked by cacti, divi-divi trees, and aloe vera plants. Ask if you can stop off at Cura di Tortuga, a natural pool that's reputed to have restorative powers. Rides are also possible in Arikok National Wildlife Park. Rates run from $35 for an hour-long trip to $65 for a three-hour tour; private rides cost slightly more.

Horseback riding on the beach.

🕐 **De Palm Tours** (✉ *L.G. Smith Blvd. 142, Oranjestad* ☎297/582–4400 or 800/766–6016 ⊕*www.depalm.com*) arranges horseback-riding excursions.

Rancho del Campo (✉ *Sombre 22E, Santa Cruz* ☎297/585–0290 ⊕*www.ranchodelcampo.com*), the first to offer rides to Natural Pool back in 1991, leads various excursions that start at $70 per person.

🕐 **Rancho Daimari** (✉ *Tanki Leendert 249, San Nicolas* ☎297/587–5674 ⊕*www.visitaruba.com/ranchodaimari*) will lead your horse to water—either at Natural Bridge or Natural Pool—in the morning or afternoon for $64 per person. The "Junior Dudes" program is tailored to young riders. There are even ATV trips.

Rancho Notorious (✉ *Boroncana, Noord* ☎297/586–0508 ⊕*www.ranchonotorious.com*) will take you on a tour of the countryside for $45, to the beach to snorkel for $120, or on a three-hour ride up to the California Lighthouse for $70. The company also organizes ATV and mountain-biking trips.

JET SKIING

If zipping through aqua-blue water at unholy speeds is your idea of fun, then renting a Jet Ski may be the way to go. Rentals are available in the water-sports centers at most hotels. Average prices for a half-hour ride are $65 for a

Kayaking in a sheltered cove.

single Jet Ski and $75 for a double. There are a few operators on the island, two of which are well regarded.

Pelican Tours & Watersports (⊠*Pelican Pier, near Holiday Inn and Playa Linda hotels, Palm Beach* ☎*297/586–3271* ⊕*www. pelican-aruba.com*) offers Jet Skis and WaveRunners.

Unique Sports of Aruba (⊠*Radisson Aruba Resort & Casino, J. E. Irausquin Blvd. 81, Palm Beach* ☎*297/586–0096* ⊕*www.visitaruba.com/uniquesports*), operating exclusively from the Radisson Resort on Palm Beach, rents single and double Jet Skis.

7

KAYAKING

Kayaking is a popular sport on Aruba, especially because the waters are so calm. It's a great way to explore the coast.

Aruba Kayak Adventure (⊠*Ponton 90, Oranjestad* ☎*297/587– 7722* ⊕*www.arubakayak.com*) has excellent half-day kayak trips, which start with a quick lesson before you paddle through caves and mangroves and along the scenic coast. The tour makes a lunch stop at De Palm Island, where snorkeling is included as part of the $99 package.

Every day except Sunday, **De Palm Tours** (⊠*L. G. Smith Blvd. 142, Oranjestad* ☎*297/582–4400 or 800/766–6016*

⊕*www.depalm.com*) offers a four-hour guided kayaking tour that includes some snorkeling. The cost, including lunch, is $99.

KITEBOARDING

★ Thanks to constant trade winds, kiteboarding (also called kitesurfing) is fast becoming a popular pastime on this tiny island. The sport involves gliding on and above the water on a small surfboard or wakeboard while hooked up to an inflatable kite. Windsurfing experience helps, and practice time on the beach is essential.

One major kiteboarding operator is **Aruba Boardsailing Productions** (⊠*L.G. Smith Blvd. 486, Palm Beach* ☎*297/ 586–3940 or 297/993–1111* ⊕*www.visitaruba.com/aruba boardsailing*). Kiteboarding rental costs are usually a reasonable $55 per day (though it may take the better part of a day to get the hang of it). Once you're proficient, you may want to participate in some of the island's freestyle tournaments and long-distance races.

Those eager to fly the friendly skies can take lessons and rent reliable equipment at Vela Windsurf's **Fisherman's Huts Windsurf Center** (⊠*L. G. Smith Blvd. 101, Palm Beach* ☎*297/586–9000 Ext. 6430 or 800/223–5443* ⊕*www. velawindsurf.com*).

PARASAILING

For about 12 exhilarating minutes, motorboats at Palm and Eagle beaches tow you up and over the waters around Aruba ($55 for a single-seater, $80 for a tandem). You can make arrangements with your hotel or through independent operators stationed on the beaches.

Caribbean Parasail (☎*297/586–0505*) is one of the island's top operators.

Working with many hotels, **Pelican Tours & Watersports** (⊠*Pelican Pier, near Holiday Inn and Playa Linda hotels, Palm Beach* ☎*297/586–3271* ⊕*www.pelican-aruba.com*) has equipment for parasailing and other outdoor activities.

Although it's best known for its diving trips, **Red Sail Sports** (⊠*J. E. Irausquin Blvd. 83* ☎*297/586–1603, 877/733–7245 in U.S.* ⊕*www.aruba-redsail.com*) will also take you parasailing.

PARKS AND PLAYGROUNDS

You can let the kids run loose in ☾ **Kibaima Miniature Village** (⊠*Kibaima 5, south of airport across Hwy. 4 from outdoor theater, Oranjestad* ☎*297/585–1830 or 297/585–1980*), a little park filled with scaled-down versions of typical Aruban houses. There are also plenty of exotic birds and animals. The park is open daily from 10 to 6, with daily 10 AM tours. The $5 admission charge for children under 12 years old and $10 fee for adults includes a tour.

☾ **Tira Koochi Park** (⊠*Savaneta 338A, Oranjestad*) is open daily from 4 PM to 6:30 PM daily. The playground is behind Prome Paso School.

SCUBA DIVING AND SNORKELING

With visibility of up to 90 feet, the waters around Aruba are excellent for snorkeling and diving. Advanced and novice divers alike will find plenty to occupy their time, as many of the most popular sites—including some interesting shipwrecks—are found in shallow waters ranging from 30 to 60 feet. Coral reefs covered with sensuously waving sea fans and eerie giant sponge tubes attract a colorful menagerie of sea life, including gliding manta rays, curious sea turtles, shy octopuses, and fish from grunts to groupers. Marine preservation is a priority on Aruba, and regulations by the Conference on International Trade in Endangered Species make it unlawful to remove coral, conch, and other marine life from the water.

Expect snorkel gear to rent for about $15 per day and trips to cost around $40. Scuba rates are around $50 for a one-tank reef or wreck dive, $65 for a two-tank dive, and $45 for a night dive. Resort courses, which offer an introduction to scuba diving, average $65 to $70. If you want to go all the way, complete open-water certification costs around $350.

OPERATORS

★ The more seasoned diving crowd might check with **Aruba Pro Dive** (⊠*Ponton 88, Noord* ☎*297/582–5520* ⊕*www.arubaprodive.com*) for special deals.

Dax Divers (⊠*Kibaima 7, Santa Cruz* ☎*297/585–1270*) has an instructor training course. Some dives are less expensive, at $40 for 40 minutes with one tank and weights. It should be noted, however, that this is not a PADI-certified operation.

DID YOU KNOW?

While windsurfers stand on a large board connected to a sail, kite surfers ride a much smaller board and are propelled by a kite that flies high in the air.

Diving one of Aruba's many wrecks.

★ **De Palm Watersports** (✉ *L.G. Smith Blvd. 142, Oranjestad* ☎ *297/582–4400 or 800/766–6016* ⊕ *www.depalm.com*) is one of the best choices for your undersea experience, and the options go beyond basic diving. You can don a helmet and walk along the ocean floor near De Palm Island, home of huge blue parrot fish. You can even do Snuba—which is like scuba diving but without the heavy air tanks—from either a boat or from an island; it costs $56.

Dive Aruba (✉ *Wilhelminastraat 8, Oranjestad* ☎ *297/582–7337* ⊕ *www.divearuba.com*) offers resort courses, certification courses, and trips to interesting shipwrecks.

Mermaid Sport Divers (✉ *Bubali 112-J, Sasaki Hwy. between low-rise and high-rise hotels, Oranjestad* ☎ *297/587–4103* ⊕ *www.scubadivers-aruba.com*) has dive packages but is not PADI-certified.

Native Divers Aruba (✉ *Koyari 1, Noord* ☎ *297/586–4763* ⊕ *www.nativedivers.com*) offers all types of dives; underwater naturalist courses are taught by PADI-certified instructors.

Pelican Tours & Watersports (✉ *Pelican Pier, near Holiday Inn and Playa Linda hotels, Palm Beach* ☎ *297/586–3271* ⊕ *www.pelican-aruba.com*) has options for divers of all levels. Novices start with midmorning classes and then move to the pool to practice what they've learned; by afternoon they put their new skills to use at a shipwreck off the coast.

Red Sail Sports (✉*J. E. Irausquin Blvd. 83, Oranjestad* ☎*297/586–1603, 877/733–7245 in U.S.* ⊕*www.redsail. com*) has courses for children and others new to scuba diving. An introductory class costs about $89.

SEAruba Fly 'n Dive (✉*Shiribana 9A, Paradera* ☎*297/587–8759* ⊕*www.se-aruba.com*), aside from the usual diving courses, can also instruct your group in rescue techniques and the finer points of underwater photography.

Unique Sports of Aruba (✉*Radisson Aruba Resort & Casino, J. E. Irausquin Blvd. 81, Palm Beach* ☎*297/586–0096 or 297/586–3900* ⊕*www.visitaruba.com/uniquesports*) lives up to its name, providing dive master, rescue, and certification courses.

WEST-SIDE DIVE SITES

Antilla **Wreck.** This German freighter, which sank off the northwest coast near Malmok Beach, is popular with both divers and snorkelers. Scuttled during World War II not long after its maiden voyage, the 400-foot-long vessel—referred to by locals as "the ghost ship"—has large compartments. You can climb into the captain's bathtub, which sits beside the wreck, for a unique photo op. Lobster, angelfish, yellowtail, and other fish swim about the wreck, which is blanketed by giant tube sponges and coral.

WORD OF MOUTH. "You can . . . hop a boat to the wreck of the *Antilla*, a World War II German freighter whose superstructure is visible from the shore. . . . Now its a neat place to snorkel as its become an artificial reef." —jacketwatch

Barcadera Reef. Only large types of coral—staghorn, elkhorn, pillar—find their niche close to this reef because the sand makes it difficult for the smaller varieties to survive. The huge (and abundant) sea fans here wave in the current.

Black Beach. The clear waters just off this beach are dotted with sea fans. The area takes its name from the rounded black stones lining the shore. It's the only bay on the island's north coast sheltered from thunderous waves, making it a safe spot for diving.

Californian **Wreck.** Although this steamer is submerged at a depth that's perfect for underwater photography, this site is safe only for advanced divers; the currents here are strong, and the waters are dangerously choppy.

Harbour Reef. Steeply sloped boulders surrounded by a multitude of soft coral formations make this a great spot for novices. The calm waters are noteworthy for their abundance of fascinating plant life.

Malmok Reef. Lobsters and stingrays are among the highlights at this bottom reef adorned by giant green, orange, and purple barrel sponges as well as leaf and brain coral. From here you can spot the *Debbie II*, a 120-foot barge that sank in 1992.

***Pedernales* Wreck.** During World War II this oil tanker was torpedoed by a German submarine. The U.S. military cut out the damaged centerpiece, towed the two remaining pieces to the States, and welded them together into a smaller vessel that eventually transported troops during the invasion of Normandy. The section that was left behind in shallow water is now surrounded by coral formations, making this a good site for novice divers. The ship's cabins, washbasins, and pipelines are exposed. The area teems with grouper and angelfish.

Skeleton Cave. Human bones found here (historians hypothesize that they're remains of ancient Arawak people) gave this dive spot its name. A large piece of broken rock forms the entrance where the cave meets the coast.

Sonesta Reef. Two downed planes are the centerpiece of this interesting dive site near Sonesta Island. Several types of brain coral abound in this sandy-bottom area.

Tugboat Wreck. Spotted eagle rays and stingrays are sometimes observed at this shipwreck at the foot of Harbour Reef, making it one of Aruba's most popular. Spectacular formations of brain, sheet, and star coral blanket the path to the wreck, which is inhabited by a pair of bright green moray eels.

EAST-SIDE DIVE SITES
***Captain Roger* Wreck.** A plethora of colorful fish swish about this old tugboat, which rests off the coast at Seroe Colorado. From shore you can swim to a steep coral reef.

Isla di Oro. A wide expanse of reef grows far out along the shallow bank, making for superb diving. You'll be treated to views of green moray eels, coral crabs, trumpet fish, and French, gray, and queen angelfish.

***Jane* Wreck.** This 200-foot freighter, lodged in an almost vertical position at a depth of 90 feet, is near the coral reef west of Palm Island. Night diving is exciting here, as the polyps emerge from the corals that grow profusely on the steel plates of the decks and cabins. Soft corals and sea fans are also abundant in the area.

Palm Island. Secluded behind clusters of mangrove, the reef system around Palm Island stretches all the way to Oranjestad. You can get close enough to touch the nurse sharks that sleep tucked into reef crevices during the day.

Punta Basora. This narrow reef stretches far into the sea off the island's easternmost point. On calm days you'll see eagle rays, stingrays, barracudas, and hammerhead sharks, as well as hawksbill and loggerhead turtles.

Shark Caves. At this site along the island's southeastern point you can swim alongside sand sharks and float past the nurse sharks sleeping under the rock outcroppings.

***Vera* Wreck.** In 1954 this freighter sank while en route to North America. The crew, saved by an Aruban captain, claimed the ship held Nazi treasures.

The Wall. From May to August, green sea turtles intent on laying their eggs abound at this steep-walled reef. You'll also spot long-branched gorgons, groupers, and burrfish swimming nearby. Close to shore, massive sheet corals are plentiful; in the upper part of the reef are colorful varieties such as black coral, star coral, and flower coral. Flitting about are brilliant damselfish, rock beauties, and porgies.

SPECTATOR SPORTS

☽ You probably won't find Arubans singing "Take Me Out to the Ball Game," but come time for soccer season (late May–November, with matches on Tuesday, Thursday, Saturday, and Sunday) or track-and-field meets, and some 3,200 spirited people pack into the **Compleho Deportivo Guillermo Prospero Trinidad** (⊠*Stadionweg, Oranjestad* ☎*297/582–9550*). Events at this complex open with the Aruban national anthem, a display of flags, and the introduction of any old-timers in the stadium. Adult admission ranges from $3 to $6, depending on whether it's a local or international competition; children get in for just over a dollar. Regardless of what's on, you won't find vendors hawking hot dogs or cotton candy. The snack bar sells such Aruban favorites as *pastechi* (meat-, cheese-, or seafood-filled turnovers) and *bitterballen* (bite-size meatballs), which you can wash down with a soda or a local Balashi beer.

SUBMARINE EXCURSIONS

Explore an underwater reef teeming with marine life without getting wet. **Atlantis Submarines** (⊠*Renaissance Marina, L. G. Smith Blvd. 82, Oranjestad* ☎*297/583–6090* ⊕*www. atlantisadventures.net*) operates a 65-foot air-conditioned sub, *Atlantis VI,* which takes 48 passengers 95 to 150 feet below the surface along Barcadera Reef ($99 per person). The company also owns the *Seaworld Explorer,* a semisubmersible that allows you to sit and view Aruba's marine habitat from 5 feet below the surface ($44 per person). Make reservations a day in advance.

TENNIS

Aruba's winds make tennis a challenge even if you have the best of backhands. Although visitors can make arrangements to play at the resorts, priority goes to guests. Some private tennis clubs can also accommodate you. Try the facilities at the **Aruba Racquet Club** (⊠*Rooisanto 21, Palm Beach* ☎*297/586–0215* ⊕*www.arc.aw*). Host to a variety of international tournaments, the club has eight courts (six lighted), as well as a swimming pool, an aerobics center, and a restaurant. Fees are $10 per hour; a lesson with a pro costs $20 for a half hour, $40 for one hour.

WINDSURFING

Aruba has all it takes for windsurfing: trade winds that average 15 knots year-round (peaking May–July), a sunny climate, and perfect azure-blue waters. With a few lessons from a certified instructor, even novices will be jibing in no time. The southwestern coast's tranquil waters make it ideal for both beginners and intermediates, as the winds are steady but sudden gusts rare. Experts will find the waters of the Atlantic, especially around Grapefield and Boca Grandi beaches, more challenging; winds are fierce and often shift without warning. Rentals average about $60 a day, and lessons range from $50 to $125. Many hotels include windsurfing in their water-sports packages, and most operators can help you arrange complete windsurfing vacations.

DID YOU KNOW?

Near-constant trade winds that average 15 knots have made Aruba a popular wind-surfing destination, especially Grapefield, Boca Grandi, Malmok, and Fisherman's Huts beaches.

Aruba Beach Villas (⊠*L.G. Smith Blvd. 462, Malmok Beach* ☎*297/586–2527, 800/320–9998 in U.S.* ⊕*www.sailboard vacations.com*) offers first-rate instruction. It's at Windsurf Village, a lodging complex created by and for windsurfers near Fisherman's Huts, a world-renowned sailing spot. Another lure for those in the know: the complex is home to one of the Caribbean's largest and best-stocked windsurfing shops.

Aruba Boardsailing Productions (⊠*L.G. Smith Blvd. 486, near Fisherman's Huts, Palm Beach* ☎*297/586–3940* ⊠*297/993–1111* ⊕*www.visitaruba.com/arubaboardsailing*) is a major windsurfing center on the island.

Pelican Adventures Tours & Watersports (⊠*Pelican Pier, near Holiday Inn and Playa Linda hotels, Palm Beach* ☎*297/ 586–3600* ⊕*www.pelican-aruba.com*) usually has rental boards and sails on hand.

Sailboard Vacations (⊠*L.G. Smith Blvd. 462, Malmok Beach* ☎*297/586–2527* ⊕*www.sailboardvacations.com*) offers complete windsurf packages, including accommodation. Equipment can be rented for $60 a day.

Trade jokes and snap photos with your fellow windsurfers at **Vela Aruba** (⊠*L.G. Smith Blvd. 101, Palm Beach* ☎*297/586–9000 Ext. 6430 or 800/223–5443* ⊕*www. velawindsurf.com*). This is *the* place to make friends. It's a major kite-surfing center as well.

Shopping

WORD OF MOUTH

"Though it may not be actually 'authentic,' I brought back lots of embroided linens. . . . Also, some of the blue Delft Dutch pottery. Aruba has an aloe factory that sells aloe products. You can schedule a tour to go though it and then make a purchase."

—KVR

SHOPPING CAN BE GOOD ON ARUBA. Although stores on the island often use the tag line DUTY-FREE, the word PRICES is usually printed underneath in much smaller letters. Cheaper rents, lower taxes, and a willingness to add smaller markups mean that Aruban prices on many luxury goods are often reasonable, but not truly duty-free. Most North Americans, who find clothing to be less expensive back home, buy perfume and jewelry; South Americans tend to shell out lots of cash on a variety of brand-name merchandise.

Aruba's souvenir and crafts stores are full of Dutch porcelains and figurines, as befits the island's heritage. Dutch cheese is a good buy (you're allowed to bring up to 10 pounds of hard cheese through U.S. customs), as are hand-embroidered linens and any products made from the native aloe-vera plant—sunburn cream, face masks, skin refreshers. Local arts and crafts run toward wood carvings and earthenware emblazoned with ARUBA: ONE HAPPY ISLAND and the like.

Island merchants are honest and pleasant. Still, if you encounter price markups, unsatisfactory service, or other shopping obstacles, call the tourist office, which will in turn contact the Aruba Merchants Association. A representative of the association will speak with the merchant on your behalf, even if the store isn't an association member.

HOW AND WHEN

It's easy to spend money in Aruba. Most stores accept American currency and Aruban florins (written as "Afl") as well as credit cards and traveler's checks. In 2007 Aruba introduced a 3% sales tax on most goods and services, which includes most purchases by tourists. Though many stores downtown advertise "duty-free" prices, Aruba is not a duty-free port, so the only duty-free prices are to be had at the airport. Good bargains are to be had for those who have a good knowledge of U.S. prices and who shop carefully. Don't try to bargain in stores, where it's considered rude to haggle. At flea markets and souvenir stands, however, you might be able to strike a deal.

Stores are open Monday through Saturday from 8:30 or 9 to 6. Some stores stay open through the lunch hour (noon to 2), and many open when cruise ships are in port on Sunday and holidays. The later you shop in downtown Oranjestad, the easier it will be to find a place to park. Also, later hours mean slightly lower temperatures. In fact,

Aruba has many popular shopping malls.

the Aruba Merchants Association is one force behind the effort to have shops stay open later, so that visitors who like to spend the day on the beach can shop in the cool of the evening.

AREAS AND MALLS

For late-night shopping, head to the **Alhambra Casino Shopping Arcade** (⊠*L.G. Smith Blvd. 47, Manchebo Beach*), which is open until midnight. Souvenir shops, boutiques, and fast-food outlets fill the arcade, which is attached to the popular casino.

Although small, the **Aquarius Mall** (⊠*Elleboogstraat 1, Oranjestad*) has some upscale shops.

Oranjestad's **Caya G.F. Betico Croes** is Aruba's chief shopping street, lined with several shops advertising "duty-free prices" (again, these are not truly duty-free), boutiques, and jewelry stores noted for the aggressiveness of their vendors on cruise-ship days.

If you blink, you might miss the good finds at **Dutch Crown Center** (⊠*L.G. Smith Blvd. 150 [some shops face Havenstraat], Oranjestad*), a tiny complex sandwiched between the major malls.

The **Holland Aruba Mall** (⊠*Havenstraat 6, Oranjestad*) houses a collection of smart shops and eateries.

Paseo Herencia (⌧*L.G. Smith Blvd., Palm Beach* ☎*297/ 586–6533*) is the newest mall in Aruba, just minutes away from the high-rise hotel area. It's all about style, and from the bell tower to the nightly dancing waters shows and the selection of restaurants, the aim here is to pull in shoppers. Offerings include Cuban cigars, the fine leather goods of Mario Hernandez, Italian denim goods at Moda & Stile, perfumes, cosmetics, and a variety of souvenir shops.

Stores at the **Port of Call Marketplace** (⌧*L.G. Smith Blvd. 17, Oranjestad*) sell fine jewelry, perfumes, low-priced liquor, batiks, crystal, leather goods, and fashionable clothing.

Five minutes from the cruise-ship terminal, the **Renaissance Mall** (⌧*L.G. Smith Blvd. 82, Oranjestad*), also known as Seaport Mall, has more than 120 stores selling merchandise to meet every taste and budget; the Crystal Casino is also here.

★ The **Royal Plaza Mall** (⌧*L.G. Smith Blvd. 94, Oranjestad*), across from the cruise-ship terminal, has cafés, a post office (open weekdays 8 to 3:30), and such stores as Nautica, Benetton, Tommy Hilfiger, and Gandelman Jewelers. There's also a Cyber Café for those who want to send e-mail and get their caffeine fix all in one stop.

The pastel-hued **Strada I and Strada II** (⌧*Klipstraat and Rifstraat, Oranjestad*) are shopping complexes in Dutch-style buildings.

SPECIALTY STORES

CIGARS

You can find fine cigars at **La Casa Del Habano** (⌧*Royal Plaza Mall, L.G. Smith Blvd. 94, Oranjestad* ☎*297/583–8509*).

At the **Cigar Emporium** (⌧*Renaissance Mall, L.G. Smith Blvd. 82, Oranjestad* ☎*297/582–5479*) the Cubans come straight from the climate-controlled humidor. Choose from Cohiba, Montecristo, Romeo y Julieta, Partagas, and more.

Superior Tobacco (⌧*L.G. Smith Blvd. 120, Oranjestad* ☎*297/ 582–3220*) is a good place to shop for stogies.

Ronchi de Cuba's Aruban Style

"Shopping has recently become tremendously advanced on Aruba," says local fashion designer Ronchi de Cuba. "We're seeing higher-end fashion that's more reasonably priced, from companies like Fendi and Gucci, and the shopping area is still growing." He says the best time to get great buys at the high-end stores is in January, when the holidays are over and the racks are being cleared for the new season.

De Cuba became involved in fashion at age 17, thanks to a high school physical-education assignment for which he taught a dance class and presented a show that incorporated theater, choreography, and fashion. After attending college in Miami, de Cuba returned to his native Aruba to work at a modeling agency. Soon after, he opened his own agency to promote local entertainment and style.

The first Ronchi de Cuba design was a haute-couture number created for Miss Aruba 1999; he has since gone on to create ready-to-wear swimwear, menswear, women's wear, and junior lines. When he's not cutting clothes, the designer travels to New York, Miami, and Paris to peek into the shops and showrooms of major designers.

De Cuba clothes are constructed of fabrics suitable for a warm climate: crepe linens, silk georgettes, and shantungs for day; brocade, wool crepe, crepe de chine, and silk chiffon for evening. Inspired by such designers as John Galliano, Dolce & Gabbana, and Prada, his collections feature playful color schemes that incorporate dark solids, bright colors, and prints. He turns out a spring-summer collection and a holiday-cruise collection each year.

Always on the cutting edge of fashion, de Cuba is also known on the island for hosting the annual International Male Model contest, featuring dozens of contestants from the Caribbean, South and Central America, the United States, the United Arab Emirates, and Europe.

Look for de Cuba's label at stores in the Seaport Village Marketplace and the Royal Plaza Mall or at his own shop—Revolution—in Oranjestad.

8

CLOTHING

★ People come to **Caperucita Raja** (⊠ *Wilhelminastraat 17, Oranjestad* ☎ *297/583–6166*) for designer baby, children's, and junior clothes, as well as a wide selection of shoes. Outfits that cost $21 here sell for more than three times that amount at Saks Fifth Avenue.

Forget to pack your intimates? **Colombia Moda** (⊠ *Wilhelminastraat 19, Oranjestad* ☎*297/582–3460*) will help complete your wardrobe with lingerie made of high-quality microfiber fabrics.

Confetti (⊠*Renaissance Mall, L.G. Smith Blvd. 82, Oranjestad* ☎*297/583–8614*) has the hottest European and American swimsuits, cover-ups, and beach essentials.

★ **Del Sol** (⊠*Royal Plaza Mall, L.G. Smith Blvd. 94, Oranjestad* ☎*297/583–8448*) is the place to buy beach accessories such as sun visors, and shirts and shorts that change colors in the sun.

Extreme Sports (⊠*Royal Plaza Mall, L.G. Smith Blvd. 94, Oranjestad* ☎*297/583–7105*) sells everything sportsaholics could ever need. Invest in a set of in-line skates or a boogie board, or pick up a backpack, bathing suit, or pair of reef walkers in funky shades.

Hunkemoller (⊠*Paseo Herencia, L.G. Smith Blvd. 382, Palm Beach*) a European chain with more than 1,000 outlets worldwide, offers everything from provocative and fashionable lingerie to sizzling beachwear that is sure to grab the attention of other beachgoers.

At **Mango** (⊠*Main St. 9, Oranjestad* ☎*297/582–9700*)—part of an international chain—you can find fashions from as far away as Spain.

Moda Actual (⊠*Caya G.F. Betico Croes 49, Oranjestad* ☎*297/583–1202*) rotates its reasonably priced, high-quality merchandise about every two months. Popular items include preshrunk cotton tank tops and T-shirts for men and women.

If the Aruban sun doesn't make your life sizzle, the sexy lingerie at **Secrets of Aruba** (⊠*Renaissance Mall, L.G. Smith Blvd. 82, Oranjestad* ☎*297/583–0897*) just might. The store also sells oils and lotions that aren't used for getting a tan.

As the many repeat customers will tell you, **Sun + Sand** (⊠*Dutch Crown Center, L.G. Smith Blvd. 150, Oranjestad* ☎*297/583–8812*) is *the* place for T-shirts, sweatshirts, polo shirts, and cover-ups.

For innovative activewear, check out **Tommy Hilfiger** (⊠*Royal Plaza Mall, L.G. Smith Blvd. 94, Oranjestad*

☎297/583–8548). Be sure to visit the Tommy Jeans store as well.

Menswear reigns supreme at **La Venezolana** (⊠*Steenweg 12, Oranjestad* ☎297/582–1444). You can find blazers and suits as well as jeans, belts, and shoes. Look for such names as Givenchy, Lee Jeans, and Van Heusen.

★ **Wulfsen & Wulfsen** (⊠*Caya G.F. Betico Croes 52, Oranjestad* ☎297/582–3823) has been one of the most highly regarded clothing stores in Aruba and the Netherlands Antilles for 30 years. It carries elegant suits for men and linen cocktail dresses for women; it's also a great place to buy Bermuda shorts.

FOOD

The clean, orderly **Kong Hing Supermarket** (⊠*L.G. Smith Blvd. 152, Bushiri* ☎297/582–5545) stocks all the comforts of home—from fresh cuts of meat to prepackaged salads. The liquor section offers everything from exotic liqueurs to familiar beers. The market, which is open Monday to Saturday 8 to 8 and Sunday 9 to 1, accepts Discover, MasterCard, and Visa for purchases of $10 or more. There's also an ATM on the premises.

The family-owned and -operated **Ling & Sons Supermarket** (⊠*Italiëstraat 26, Eagle Beach* ☎297/583–2370 ⊕*www. visitaruba.com/ling&sons*) is one of the island's top grocers. In addition to a wide variety of foods, there's a bakery, a deli, a butcher shop, and a well-stocked "liquortique." If you e-mail ahead, the store can have a package of essential foodstuffs delivered to your hotel room. The market is open Monday to Saturday 8 to 8 and Sunday 9 to 1. Before the December holidays, the store sometimes stays open an hour later on weekdays.

GIFTS AND SOUVENIRS

★ **Art & Tradition Handicrafts** (⊠*Caya G.F. Betico Croes 30, Oranjestad* ☎297/583–6534 ⊠*Royal Plaza Mall, L.G. Smith Blvd. 94, Oranjestad* ☎297/582–7862) sells intriguing souvenirs. Buds from the *mopa mopa* tree are boiled to form a resin, which is colored using vegetable dyes, then stretched by hand and mouth. Tiny pieces form intricate designs—these are truly unusual gifts.

The **Artistic Boutique** (⊠*Caya G. F. Betico Croes 25, Oranjestad* ☎297/582–3142 ⊠*Wyndham Aruba Beach Resort & Casino, J.E. Irausquin Blvd. 77* ☎297/586–4466 Ext. 3508 ⊠*Renaissance Mall, L.G. Smith Blvd. 82,*

Small, owner-operated souvenir shops abound.

Oranjestad ☎297/583–2567 ✉Holiday Inn SunSpree Aruba Beach Resort & Casino, J.E. Irausquin Blvd. 230 ☎297/583–3383) has been in business for more than 30 years. It's known for its Giuseppe Armani figurines from Italy; Aruban hand-embroidered linens; gold and silver jewelry; and porcelain and pottery from Spain.

El Bohio (✉*Port of Call Marketplace, L.G. Smith Blvd. 17, Oranjestad* ☎*297/582–9178*) will charm you with its wooden-hut displays holding Arawak-style pottery, Dutch shoes, and wind chimes. You can also find classic leather handbags.

Creative Hands (✉*Socotorolaan 5, Oranjestad* ☎*297/583–5665*) sells porcelain and ceramic miniatures of *cunucu* (country) houses and divi-divi trees, but the store's real draw is its exquisite Japanese dolls.

For pottery lovers, **Kwa Kwa** (✉*Port of Call Marketplace, L.G. Smith Blvd. 17, Oranjestad* ☎*297/583–9471*) is a paradise. There are wind chimes, pottery, and knickknacks galore—all made of ceramic, of course. Other items include embroidered bags.

While you wait 30 minutes for your film to be developed or your digital images to be printed at **New Face Photo** (✉*Dutch Crown Center, Havenstraat 27, Oranjestad* ☎*297/582–9510*), you can shop for gifts.

Clothes from Aruba and Indonesia, hand-painted mobiles, and bamboo wind chimes are among the goodies at **Tropical Wave** (⊠*Port of Call Marketplace, L.G. Smith Blvd. 17, Oranjestad* ☎*297/582–1905*).

At **Vibes** (⊠*Royal Plaza Mall, L.G. Smith Blvd. 93, Oranjestad* ☎*297/583–7949*), treat yourself to a Monte Crisco or Cohiba cigar, and pick up souvenirs such as postcards, picture frames, and T-shirts.

HOUSEWARES

Locals swear by **Decor Home Fashions** (⊠*Steenweg 14, Oranjestad* ☎*297/582–6620*), which sells sheets, towels, place mats, and other linens imported from Italy, Germany, Holland, Portugal, and the United States.

JEWELRY

Filling 6,000 square feet of space, **Boolchand's** (⊠*Renaissance Mall, L.G. Smith Blvd. 82, Oranjestad* ☎*297/583–0147*) sells jewelry and watches. It also stocks leather goods, cameras, and electronics.

If green fire is your passion, **Colombian Emeralds** (⊠*Renaissance Mall, L.G. Smith Blvd. 82, Oranjestad* ☎*297/583–6238*) has a dazzling array. There are also fine European watches.

For all that glitters, head to **Diamonds International** (⊠*Port of Call Marketplace, L.G. Smith Blvd. 17, Oranjestad* ☎*800/515–3935*).

Gandelman Jewelers (⊠*Royal Plaza Mall, L.G. Smith Blvd. 94, Oranjestad* ☎*297/583–4433*) sells Gucci and Rolex watches at reasonable prices. The store also has gold bracelets and a full line of Lladro figurines.

★ Find one-of-a-kind silver pieces at **Grace Silver & Beyond** (⊠*Seaport Marketplace 13, L.G. Smith Blvd. 9, Oranjestad* ☎*297/588–6262*).

Kenro Jewelers (⊠*Renaissance Mall, L.G. Smith Blvd. 82, Oranjestad* ☎*297/583–4847 or 297/583–3171*) has two stores in the same mall, attesting to the popularity of its stock of bracelets and necklaces from Ramon Leopard; jewelry by Arando, Micheletto, and Blumei; and various brands of watches. There are also six other locations, including some in major hotels.

Precious pearls add lustre to many of the pretty items at **Pearl Gems Fine Jewelry** (⊠*L.G. Smith Blvd. 90–92, Oranjestad* ☎*297/588–4927*).

Beyond T-Shirts and Key Chains

You can't go wrong with baseball caps, refrigerator magnets, beer mugs, sweatshirts, T-shirts, key chains, and other local logo merchandise. You won't go broke buying these items, either.

Budget for a major purchase. If souvenirs are all about keeping the memories alive in the long haul, plan ahead to shop for something really special—a work of art, a rug or something else hand-crafted, or a major accessory for your home. One major purchase will stay with you far longer than a dozen tourist trinkets.

Add to your collection. Whether antiques, used books, salt and pepper shakers, or ceramic frogs are your thing, start looking in the first day or two. Chances are you'll want to scout around and then go back to some of the first shops you visited before you hand over your credit card.

Get guarantees in writing. Is the vendor making promises? Ask him to put them in writing.

Anticipate a shopping spree. If you think you might buy breakables, include a length of bubble wrap. Pack a large tote bag in your suitcase in case you need extra space. Don't fill your suitcase to bursting before you leave home. Or include some old clothing that you can leave behind to make room for new acquisitions.

Know before you go. Study prices at home on items you might consider buying while you're away. Otherwise you won't recognize a bargain when you see one.

Plastic, please. Especially if your purchase is pricey and you're looking for authenticity, it's always smart to pay with a credit card. If a problem arises later and the merchant can't or won't resolve it, the credit-card company may help you out.

LEATHER GOODS

Alivio (⊠*Steenweg 12-1, Oranjestad*) has shoes for men, women, and children. Whether you're walking around town by day or dressing up for dinner at night, you can find something suitable in this Oranjestad shop. Look for Birkenstock from Germany, Piedro and Wolky from Holland, and Mephisto from France.

Ferragamo (⊠*Emmastraat 1, Oranjestad* ☎*297/582–8218*) has a popular boutique behind Royal Plaza Mall.

If you get lucky, you can catch one of the year's big sales (one is held the first week in December, the other the first week in February) at **Gucci** (⊠*Renaissance Mall, L.G. Smith*

ARUBA TRADING
COMPANY

Blvd. 82, Oranjestad ☎*297/583–3952*), when prices are slashed on handbags, luggage, wallets, shoes, watches, belts, and ties.

Mario Hernandez (✉*Paseo Herencia, L.G. Smith Blvd. 382, Palm Beach* ☎*297/586–0300*), a Colombian designer, offers some spectacular examples of quality leatherwork in his handbags, jackets, shoes, and accessories.

LUXURY GOODS

For perfumes, cosmetics, clothing, and leather goods (including Bally shoes), stop in at **Aruba Trading Company** (✉*Caya G.F. Betico Croes 12, Oranjestad* ☎*297/582–2602*), which has been in business for nearly 75 years.

★ **Little Switzerland** (✉*Caya G.F. Betico Croes 14, Oranjestad* ☎*297/582–1192* ✉*Royal Plaza Mall, L.G. Smith Blvd. 94, Oranjestad* ☎*297/583–4057*), the St. Thomas–based giant, is the place to go for porcelain, crystal, and fine tableware. You can also find good buys on Omega and Rado watches, Swarovski and Baccarat crystal, and Lladro figurines.

At **Weitnauer** (✉*Caya G.F. Betico Croes 29, Oranjestad* ☎*297/582–2790*) you can find specialty Lenox items as well as a wide range of fragrances.

PERFUMES

Aruba Trading Company, Little Switzerland, and Weitnauer are also known for their extensive fragrance offerings (*see Luxury Goods, above*).

A venerated name in Aruba, **J.L. Penha & Sons** (✉ *Caya G.F. Betico Croes 11/13, Oranjestad* ☎*297/582–4160 or 297/582–4161*) sells high-end perfumes and cosmetics. It stocks such brands as Cartier, Dior, and Givenchy.

Maggy's (✉*Renaissance Maill, L.G. Smith Blvd. 82, Oranjestad* ☎*297/583–6108* ✉*Paseo Herencia, L.G. Smith Blvd 382, Palm Beach* ☎*297/586–6506*), sells a selection of high-end perfumes and cosmetics. Best of all, there is a full-service salon at both locations.

Travel Smart Aruba

GETTING HERE & AROUND

We're proud of our Web site: Fodors.com is a great place to begin any journey. Scan Travel Wire for suggested itineraries, travel deals, restaurant and hotel openings, and other up-to-the-minute info. Check out Booking to research prices and book plane tickets, hotel rooms, rental cars, and vacation packages. Head to Talk for on-the-ground pointers from travelers who frequent our message boards. You can also link to loads of other travel-related resources.

Aruba is a small island, so it's virtually impossible to get lost when exploring. Most activity takes place in and around Oranjestad or in the two main hotel areas, which are designated as the "low-rise" and "high-rise" areas. Main roads on the island are generally excellent, but getting to some of the more secluded beaches or historic sites will involve driving on unpaved tracks. Though Aruba is an arid island, there are periods of heavy rain, and it is best to avoid exploring the national park or other wilderness areas during these times, since roads can become flooded, and muddy conditions can make driving treacherous.

■TIP➔Ask the local tourist board about hotel and local transportation packages that include tickets to major museum exhibits or other special events.

▌ BY AIR

Aruba is 2½ hours from Miami, 4½ hours from New York, and 9½ hours from Amsterdam. The flight from New York to San Juan, Puerto Rico, takes 3½ hours; from Miami to San Juan it's 1½ hours; and from San Juan to Aruba it's just over an hour. Shorter still is the ¼- to ½-hour hop (depending on whether you take a prop or a jet plane) from Curaçao to Aruba.

Airlines and Airports Airline and Airport Links.com (⊕*www. airlineandairportlinks.com*) has links to many of the world's airlines and airports.

Airline-Security Issues Transportation Security Administration (⊕*www.tsa.gov*) has answers for almost every question that might come up.

AIRPORTS

Aruba's Aeropuerto Internacional Reina Beatrix (Queen Beatrix International Airport, AUA), near the island's south coast, is a modern, passenger-friendly facility.

Airport Information Aeropuerto Internacional Reina Beatrix (☎*297/582–4800* ⊕*www.airport aruba.com*).

GROUND TRANSPORTATION

A taxi from the airport to most hotels takes about 20 minutes. It will cost $17 to get to the hotels along Eagle Beach, $20 to the high-rise hotels on Palm Beach, and $10 to the hotels downtown (rates are a few dollars higher at night). You'll find a taxi stand right outside the baggage-claim area.

FLIGHTS

There are nonstop flights to Aruba from Boston, Charlotte, Chicago (seasonal service), Houston, Miami, Newark, New York–JFK, and Philadelphia. Canadian travelers may fly nonstop during high travel season but must connect through the United States or Caracas, Venezuela, at other times.

Checking in, paying departure taxes (if they aren't included in your ticket), clearing security, and boarding can take time on Aruba. Because security has gotten tighter, get to the airport at least three hours ahead of time. You may be randomly selected for inspection of your carry-on baggage at the gate. Regulations prohibit packing certain items in your carry-on luggage, including matches, lighters, and handheld radios. Check with your hotel concierge before packing to return home.

Airline Contacts Air Canada (297/582–6401 on Aruba, 888/247–2262 in North America www.aircanada.com). **American Airlines** (297/582–2700 on Aruba, 800/433–7300 www.aa.com). **Continental Airlines** (297/588–0044 on Aruba, 800/523–3273 for U.S. and Mexico reservations, 800/231–0856 for international reservations www.continental.com). **Delta Airlines** (297/588–0044 on Aruba, 800/221–1212 for U.S. reservations, 800/241–4141 for international reservations www.delta.com). **Dutch**

> **AIRLINE TIP**
>
> If you have an afternoon flight, check in your bags early in the morning (keep a change of clothes in a carry-on), then go back to the beach for one last lunch, returning to the airport an hour before your flight departs. It makes for much easier traveling, saves time, and you get your last beach fix.

Antilles Express (599/717–0808 www.flydae.com). **jetBlue** (800/ 538–2583 www.jetblue.com). **KLM** (297/582–3546 on Aruba, 31/20–4–747–747 in Amsterdam www.klm.com). **Northwest Airlines** (800/225–2525 www.nwa.com). **Spirit Airlines** (800/772–7117 or 586/791–7300 www.spiritair.com). **United Airlines** (297/588–6544 on Aruba, 800/538–2929 in North America www.united.com). **US Airways** (297/800–1580 on Aruba, 800/428–4322 for U.S. and Canada reservations, 800/622–1015 for international reservations www. usairways.com).

▮ BY BUS

Each day, from 6 AM to midnight, buses make hourly trips between the beach hotels and downtown Oranjestad. The one-way fare is $1.25, and the round-trip fare is $2.25. Exact change is preferred. Buses also run down the coast from Oranjestad to San Nicolas for the same fare. Contact the Aruba Tourism Authority for schedules. Buses run from the airport terminal to hotels every 15 minutes during the day until 8 PM, and once an hour from 8:40 PM to 12:40 AM.

▌ BY CAR

Most of Aruba's major attractions are fairly easy to find; others you'll happen upon only by sheer luck (or with an Aruban friend). International traffic signs and Dutch-style traffic signals (with an extra light for a turning lane) can be misleading if you're not used to them; use extreme caution, especially at intersections, until you grasp the rules of the road. Speed limits are rarely posted, but are usually 80 kph (50 mph) in the countryside.

GASOLINE

Gas prices average a little more than 80¢ a liter (roughly ¼ gallon), which is reasonable by Caribbean standards. Stations are plentiful in and near Oranjestad, San Nicolas, and Santa Cruz and near the major high-rise hotels on the western coast. All take cash, and most take major credit cards. Unlike in the U.S., gas prices are not posted prominently, since they are fixed and the same at all stations.

PARKING

There aren't any parking meters in downtown Oranjestad, and finding an open spot is very difficult. Try the lot on Caya G. F. Betico Croes across from the First National Bank, the one on Havenstraat near the Chez Matilde restaurant, or the one on Emanstraat near the water tower. Rates average $1.25 an hour, but some charge almost twice that.

RENTAL CARS

In Aruba you must meet the minimum age requirements of each rental service (Budget, for example, requires drivers to be over 25; Avis, over 23; and Hertz, over 21). A signed credit-card slip or a cash deposit of $500 is required. Rates for unlimited mileage are between $35 and $65 a day, with local agencies generally offering lower rates. Insurance is available starting at about $10 per day. Try to make reservations before arriving, and opt for a four-wheel-drive vehicle if you plan to explore the island.

Contacts Avis (⊠*Kolibristraat 14, Oranjestad* ☎*297/582–8787 or 800/522–9696* ⊕*www.avis. com* ⊠*Airport* ☎*297/582–5496*). **Budget** (⊠*Kolibristraat 1, Oranjestad* ☎*297/582–8600 or 800/472–3325* ⊕*www.budget. com*). **Economy** (⊠*Kolibristraat 5, Oranjestad* ☎*297/582–5176* ⊕*www.economyaruba.com*). **Hedwina Car Rental** (⊠*Bubali 93A, Noord* ☎*297/587–6442* ⊠*Airport* ☎*297/583–0880*). **Hertz** (⊠*Sabana Blanco 35, near airport* ☎*297/582–1845 or 800/654–3001* ⊕*www.hertz. com* ⊠*Airport* ☎*297/582–9112*). **National** (⊠*Tanki Leendert 170, Noord* ☎*297/587–1967 or 800/227–7368* ⊕*www.nationalcar. com* ⊠*Airport* ☎*297/582–5451*). **Thrifty** (⊠*Balashi 65, Santa Cruz* ☎*297/585–5300* ⊕*www.thrifty.com* ⊠*Airport* ☎*297/583–5335*).

RENTAL CAR INSURANCE

Everyone who rents a car wonders whether the insurance that the rental companies offer is worth the expense. No one—including us—

has a simple answer. If you own a car, your personal auto insurance may cover a rental to some degree, though not all policies protect you abroad; always read your policy's fine print. If you don't have auto insurance, then seriously consider buying the collision- or loss-damage waiver (CDW or LDW) from the car-rental company, which eliminates your liability for damage to the car. Some credit cards offer CDW coverage, but it's usually supplemental to your own insurance and rarely covers SUVs, minivans, or luxury models. If your coverage is secondary, you may still be liable for loss-of-use costs from the car-rental company. But no credit-card insurance is valid unless you use that card for *all* transactions, from reserving to paying the final bill. It's sometimes cheaper to buy insurance as part of your general travel insurance policy.

ROADSIDE EMERGENCIES

Discuss with the rental-car agency what to do in the case of an emergency. Make sure you understand what your insurance covers and what it doesn't; let someone at your accommodation know where you are heading and when you plan to return. If you find yourself stranded, hail a taxi or speak to the locals, who may have some helpful advice about finding your way to a phone or a bus stop. Keep emergency numbers with you, just in case. Because Aruba is such a small island, you should never panic if you have car trouble; it's likely you'll be within relatively easy walking distance of a populated area.

ROAD CONDITIONS

Aside from the major highways, the island's winding roads are poorly marked (although the situation is slowly improving). Keep an eye out for rocks and other debris when driving on remote roads.

RULES OF THE ROAD

Driving here is on the right side of the road, American-style. Despite the laid-back ways of locals, when they get behind the steering wheel they often speed and take liberties with road rules, especially outside the more heavily traveled Oranjestad and hotel areas. Keep a watchful eye for passing cars and for vehicles coming out of side roads. The maximum speed is 40 mph (60 kph), 25 mph (40 kph) through settlements, and limits, as well as the use of seat belts, are enforced.

▌ BY TAXI

There's a dispatch office at the airport; you can also flag down taxis on the street (look for license plates with a "TX" tag). Rates are fixed (i.e., there are no meters; the rates are set by the government and displayed on a chart), though you and the driver should agree on the fare before your ride begins. Add $2 to the fare after midnight and $2 to $4 on Sunday and holidays. An hour-long island tour costs about $40, with up to four people. Rides into town from Eagle Beach run about $8; from Palm Beach, about $13.

Contact Airport Taxi Dispatch (☎ *297/582–2116*).

ESSENTIALS

■ ACCOMMODATIONS

In Aruba hotels usually add an 11% service charge to the bill and collect 8% in government taxes for a whopping total of 19% on top of quoted rates.

Most hotels and other lodgings require you to give your credit-card details before they will confirm your reservation. If you don't feel comfortable e-mailing this information, ask if you can fax it (some places even prefer faxes). However you book, get confirmation in writing and have a copy of it handy when you check in.

Be sure you understand the hotel's cancellation policy. Some places allow you to cancel without any kind of penalty—even if you prepaid to secure a discounted rate—if you cancel at least 24 hours in advance. Others require you to cancel a week in advance or penalize you the cost of one night. Small inns and B&Bs are most likely to require you to cancel far in advance. Most hotels allow children under a certain age to stay in their parents' room at no extra charge, but others charge for them as extra adults; find out the cutoff age for discounts.

■TIP➔Assume that hotels operate on the European Plan (EP, no meals) unless we specify that they use the Breakfast Plan (BP, with full breakfast), Continental Plan (CP, continental breakfast), Full American Plan (FAP, all meals), or Modified

FODORS.COM

Before your trip, be sure to check out what other travelers are saying in Talk on www.fodors.com.

American Plan (MAP, breakfast and dinner), or are all-inclusive (AI, all meals and most activities).

For lodging price categories, consult the price charts found near the beginning of each chapter.

APARTMENT AND HOUSE RENTALS

Apartments and time-share condos are common in Aruba. So if you are looking for more space for your family or group to spread out in (and especially if you want to have access to a kitchen to make some meals), this can be a very budget-friendly option in Aruba. The money you save can be used for more dining and activities. Many time-share resorts are full-service, offering the same range of water sports and other activities as any other resort. And some regular resorts also have a time-share component.

Contacts Forgetaway (⊕*www.forgetaway.weather.com*). **Home Away** (☎*512/493–0382 in U.S.* ⊕*www.homeaway.com*). **Villas International** (☎*415/499–9490 or 800/221–2260 in U.S.* ⊕*www.villasintl.com*).

HOTELS

Aruba is a major tourist destination, and offers a variety of hotel types. Most hotels are located in two stretches, the low-rise hotels in a stretch along Druif Beach and Eagle Beach and the high-rise hotels on a stretch of Palm Beach. With a few exceptions, the hotels in the high-rise area tend to be larger and more expensive than their low-rise counterparts, but they usually offer a wider range of services.

▌ADDRESSES

"Informal" might best describe Aruban addresses. Sometimes the street designation is in English (as in J.E. Irausquin Blvd.), other times in Dutch (as in Wilhelminastraat); sometimes it's not specified whether something is a boulevard or a *straat* (street) at all. Street numbers follow street names, and postal codes aren't used. In rural areas, you might have to ask a local for directions—and be prepared for such instructions as "Take a right at the market, then a left where you see the big divi-divi tree."

▌COMMUNICATIONS

INTERNET

Most hotels now have some kind of Internet connection. In Oranjestad, Internet Planet is the place to check your e-mail. It's in the Renaissance Mall.

Contacts Cybercafes (⊕*www. cybercafes.com*).

HOTEL TIPS

Remember the taxes. Taxes and service charges add up to 19% to your hotel.

Avoid peak season (May through October). Rates often double in peak season, and the beaches are also more crowded.

Book in advance. Many hotels and attractions offer Internet-only specials that can mean a savings of more than 10%.

Take the bus. Most places of interest to tourists are located along the route between the high-rise hotels and Oranjestad.

Consider a room without an ocean view. There can be a huge price difference between a room with a view and one with no view.

Do you really need all-inclusive? While AI resorts might seem to be a better bargain, they limit your dining and nightlife options.

Consider your options. There are many large luxury resorts, but smaller resorts are cheaper, less crowded, and offer more personal service.

Not sure where to stay? Aruba Tourism Authority has a comprehensive list of accommodations (⊕*www.aruba.com*) and the staff are always ready to help in finding accommodations to suit any budget.

PHONES

To call Aruba direct from the United States, dial 011–297, followed by the seven-digit number in Aruba. International, direct, and operator-assisted calls from Aruba to all countries in the world are possible via hotel operators or from the Government Long Distance Telephone, Telegraph, and Radio Office (SETAR), in the post-office building in Oranjestad. When making calls on Aruba, simply dial the seven-digit number. AT&T customers can dial 800–8000 from special phones at the cruise dock and in the airport's arrival and departure halls and charge calls to their credit card. From other phones dial 121 to contact the SETAR international operator to place a collect or AT&T calling-card call. Local calls from pay phones, which accept both local currency and phone cards, cost 25¢. Business travelers or vacationers who need to be in regular contact with their families at home can rent an international cell phone from the concierge in most hotels or at some local electronics stores.

CALLING WITHIN THE DESTINATION

To make local calls, dial the seven-digit number.

CALLING OUTSIDE THE DESTINATION

To make calls to destinations outside Aruba, dial 0, then 1, the area code, and the number.

CALLING CARDS

The cheapest way to phone home is by using a phone card to dial direct. You can buy phone cards at SETAR offices, newsagents, super-

CELL PHONE TIPS

You can purchase a cheap cell phone at numerous outlets and simply "top-up" (pay as you go). Incoming calls are free, so have your family call you to save on exorbitant island rates and huge roaming charges. Not all cell phones from home will work in Aruba (some do, but you never know which ones until you're actually on-island), even if the phone company tells you it does.

markets, and some pharmacies and gas stations.

MOBILE PHONES

Aruba has excellent cellular coverage, and there are only a few remote spots where coverage is spotty. Both SETAR and Digicel offer rental phones, but take note of the cost, as the rental charges and deposit may make purchasing a cheap phone a better choice, especially if you are staying more than a week. Most U.S.–based GSM and CDMA cell phones work on Aruba.

If you have a multiband phone (some countries use frequencies different from those used in the United States) and your service provider uses the world-standard GSM network (as do T-Mobile, Cingular, and Verizon), you can probably use your phone abroad. Roaming fees can be steep. And overseas you normally pay the toll charges for incoming calls. It's almost always cheaper to send a text message than to make a call.

If you just want to make local calls, consider buying a new SIM card (note that your provider may have to unlock your phone for you to use a different SIM card) and a pre-paid service plan in the destination. You'll then have a local number and can make local calls at local rates. If your trip is extensive, you could also simply buy a new cell phone in your destination, as the initial cost will be offset over time.

■TIP➜If you travel internationally frequently, save one of your old mobile phones or buy a cheap one on the Internet; ask your cell-phone company to unlock it for you, and take it with you as a travel phone, buying a new SIM card with pay-as-you-go service in each destination.

Contacts Aruba Cellular (☎ 297/563–1500 ⊕ www.arubacellular.com). **Aruba Discount Cell** (☎ 297/733–9039 ⊕ www.arubadiscountcell.com). **Digicel** (☎ 297/522–2222 ⊕ www.digicelaruba.com). **SETAR** (☎ 297/525–1000 ⊕ www.setar.aw).

❚ CUSTOMS AND DUTIES

You can bring up to 1 liter of spirits, 3 liters of beer, or 2.25 liters of wine per person, and up to 200 cigarettes or 50 cigars into Aruba. You don't need to declare the value of gifts or other items, although customs officials may inquire about large items or large quantities of goods and charge (at their discretion) an import tax of 7.5% to 22% on items worth more than $230. Meat, birds, and illegal substances are forbidden. You may be

asked to provide written verification that plants are free of diseases. If you're traveling with pets, bring a veterinarian's note attesting to their good health.

Aruba Information Aruba Customs Office (☎ 297/582–1800).

U.S. Information U.S. Customs and Border Protection (⊕ www.cbp.gov).

❚ EATING OUT

Unless otherwise noted, the restaurants listed in this guide are open daily for lunch and dinner.

Aruba offers a startling variety of eating options thanks to the tourist trade, with choices ranging from upscale to simple roadside dining. The island is also a particularly family-friendly destination, so bringing the kids along is rarely a problem, and many restaurants offer children's menus. Arubans love their meat, as shown by the ubiquity of steak joints, so vegetarians may be left feeling that everyone on the island is a carnivore;

however, most kitchens are able to create a special vegetarian meal upon request if there is no vegetarian option listed on the menu.

ARUBAN CUISINE

Aruba shares many of its traditional foods with Bonaire and Curaçao. These dishes are a fusion of the various influences that have shaped the culture of the islands. Proximity to mainland South America means that many traditional snack and breakfast foods of Venezuelan origin, such as empanadas (a fried cornmeal dumpling filled with ground meat), are widely found. The Dutch influence is evident in the fondness for cheese of all sorts, but especially Gouda. Keshi Yena, ground meat with seasonings and wrapped in cheese before baking, is a national obsession.

If there is one thread that unites the cuisines of the Caribbean it is cornmeal, and Arubans love nothing more than a side of *funchi* (like a thick polenta) or a *pan bati* (a fried cornmeal pancake) to make a traditional meal complete. Though Aruban cuisine is not by nature spicy, it is almost always accompanied by a small bowl of spicy pika (a condiment of fiery hot peppers and onions in vinegar). An abundance of seafood means that seafood is the most popular protein on the island, and it has been said that if there were an Aruban national dish it would be the catch of the day.

PAYING

Most major credit cards (Visa, American Express, Diners Club, Discover, and MasterCard) are accepted in restaurants.

For guidelines on tipping see Tipping, below.

RESERVATIONS AND DRESS

We only mention reservations when they are essential (there's no other way you'll ever get a table) or when they are not accepted. We mention dress only when men are required to wear a jacket or a jacket and tie.

WINES, BEER, AND SPIRITS

Arubans have a great love for wine, so even small supermarkets have a fairly good selection of European and South American wines at prices that are reasonable by Caribbean standards. The beer of choice in Aruba is the island-brewed Balashi, though many also favor the deliciously crisp Amstel Bright, which is brewed on nearby Curaçao.

▌ ELECTRICITY

Aruba runs on a 110-volt cycle, the same as in the United States; outlets are usually the two-prong variety. Total blackouts are rare, and most large hotels have backup generators.

▌ EMERGENCIES

The number to call in case of emergency—911—is the same as in the U.S.

▌ HEALTH

As a rule, water is pure and food is wholesome in hotels and local restaurants throughout Aruba, but be cautious when buying food from street vendors. And just as you would at home, wash or peel all fruits and vegetables before eating them. Traveler's diarrhea, caused by consuming contaminated water, unpasteurized milk and milk products, and unrefrigerated food, isn't a big problem—unless it happens to you. So watch what you eat, especially at outdoor buffets in the hot sun. Make sure cooked food is hot and cold food has been properly refrigerated.

The major health risk is sunburn or sunstroke. A long-sleeve shirt, a hat, and long pants or a beach wrap are essential on a boat, for midday at the beach, and whenever you go out sightseeing. Use sunscreen with an SPF of at least 15—especially if you're fair—and apply it liberally on your nose, ears, and other sensitive and exposed areas. Make sure the sunscreen is waterproof if you're engaging in water sports. Always limit your sun time for the first few days and drink plenty of liquids. Limit intake of caffeine and alcohol, which hasten dehydration.

Mosquitoes and flies can be bothersome, so pack strong repellent (the ones that contain DEET or Picaridin are the most effective). The strong trade winds are a relief in the subtropical climate, but don't hang your bathing suit on a balcony—it will probably blow away. Help Arubans conserve water and energy: turn off air-conditioning when you leave your room, and don't let water run unattended.

Don't fly within 24 hours of scuba diving. In an emergency, Air Ambulance, run by Richard Rupert, will fly you to Curaçao at a low altitude if you need to get to a decompression chamber.

OVER-THE-COUNTER REMEDIES

There are a number of pharmacies and stores selling simple medications throughout the island (including at most hotels), and virtually anything obtainable in North America is available in Aruba.

SHOTS AND MEDICATIONS

Health Warnings **National Centers for Disease Control & Prevention** (*CDC* ☏ *877/394–8747 international travelers' health line* ⊕ *www.cdc.gov/ travel*). **World Health Organization** (*WHO* ⊕ *www.who.int*).

❚ HOURS OF OPERATION

Bank hours are weekdays 8:15 to 5:45, with some branches closing for lunch from noon to 1. The Caribbean Mercantile Bank at the airport is open Saturday 9 to 4 and Sunday 9 to 1. The central post office in Oranjestad, catercorner from the San Francisco Church, is open weekdays 7:30 to noon and 1 to 4:30. Shops are generally open Monday through Saturday 8:30 to 6. Some stores close for lunch from noon to 2. Many shops also open when cruise ships are in port on Sunday and holidays.

HOLIDAYS

Aruba's official holidays are New Year's Day, Good Friday, Easter Sunday, and Christmas, as well as Betico Croes Day (January 25), National Anthem and Flag Day (March 18), Queen's Day (April 30), Labor Day (May 1), and Ascension Day (May 1 in 2008, May 21 in 2009).

MAIL

From Aruba to the United States or Canada a letter costs Afl1.40 (about 80¢) and a postcard costs Afl.60 (35¢). Expect it to take one to two weeks. When addressing letters to Aruba, don't worry about the lack of formal addresses or postal codes; the island's postal service knows where to go.

If you need to send a package in a hurry, there are a few options. The Federal Express office across from the airport offers overnight service to the United States if you get your package in before 3 PM. Another big courier service is UPS, and there are also several smaller local courier services that provide international deliveries, most of them open weekdays 9 to 5. Check the local phone book for details.

SHIPPING PACKAGES

Federal Express service is available in downtown Oranjestad.

Contacts FedEx (✉*Browninvest Financial Center, Wayaca 31-A, Oranjestad* ☎*297/592–9039*). **UPS** (✉*Rockefellerstraat 3, Oranjestad* ☎*297/582–8646*).

MONEY

Arubans happily accept U.S. dollars virtually everywhere. That said, there's no real need to exchange money, except for necessary pocket change (for soda machines or pay phones). The official currency is the Aruban florin (Afl), also called the guilder, which is made up of 100 cents. Silver coins come in denominations of 1, 2½, 5, 10, 25, and 50 (the square one) cents. Paper currency comes in denominations of 5, 10, 25, 50, and 100 florins.

Prices quoted throughout this book are in U.S. dollars unless otherwise noted.

Prices throughout this guide are given for adults. Substantially reduced fees are almost always available for children, students, and senior citizens.

ATMS AND BANKS

If you need fast cash, you'll find ATMs that accept international cards (and dispense cash in both U.S. and local currency) at banks in Oranjestad, at the major malls, and along the roads leading to the hotel strip.

Banks RBTT Bank (✉*Caya G. F. Betico Croes 89, Oranjestad* ☎*297/582–1515*). **Caribbean Mercantile Bank** (✉*Caya G. F. Betico Croes 5, Oranjestad* ☎*297/582–3118*).

CREDIT CARDS

Throughout this guide, the following abbreviations are used: **AE**, American Express; **DC**, Diners Club; **MC**, MasterCard; and **V**, Visa.

It's a good idea to inform your credit-card company before you travel, especially if you're going abroad and don't travel internationally very often. Otherwise, the credit-card company might put a hold on your card owing to unusual activity—not a good thing halfway through your trip. Record all your credit-card numbers—as well as the phone numbers to call if your cards are lost or stolen—in a safe place, so you're prepared should something go wrong. Both MasterCard and Visa have general numbers you can call (collect if you're abroad) if your card is lost, but you're better off calling the number of your issuing bank, since MasterCard and Visa usually just transfer you to your bank; your bank's number is usually printed on your card.

If you plan to use your credit card for cash advances, you'll need to apply for a PIN at least two weeks before your trip. Although it's usually cheaper (and safer) to use a credit card abroad for large purchases (so you can cancel payments or be reimbursed if there's a problem), note that some credit-card companies *and* the banks that issue them add substantial percentages to all foreign transactions, whether they're in a foreign currency or not. Check on these fees before leaving home, so there won't be any surprises when you get the bill.

Reporting Lost Cards American Express (☎ *800/528-4800 in U.S., 336/393-1111 collect from abroad* ⊕ *www.americanexpress.com*). **MasterCard** (☎ *800/627-8372 in U.S., 636/722-7111 collect from abroad* ⊕ *www.mastercard.com*). **Visa** (☎ *800/847-2911 in U.S., 410/581-9994 collect from abroad* ⊕ *www.visa.com*).

CURRENCY EXCHANGE
At this writing exchange rates were Afl1.79 to the U.S. dollar and Afl1.43 to the Canadian dollar. Stores, hotels, and restaurants converted at Afl1.80; supermarkets and gas stations at Afl1.75. The Dutch Antillean florin—used

on Bonaire and Curaçao—isn't accepted here. Since U.S. dollars are universally accepted, few people exchange money.

Currency Conversion Google (⊕ *www.google.com*). **Oanda. com** (⊕ *www.oanda.com*). **XE.com** (⊕ *www.xe.com*).

▌ PACKING

Dress on Aruba is generally casual. Bring loose-fitting clothing made of natural fabrics to see you through days of heat and humidity. Pack a beach cover-up, both to protect yourself from the sun and to provide something to wear to and from your hotel room. Bathing suits and immodest attire are frowned upon away from the beach. A sun hat is advisable, but you don't have to pack one—inexpensive straw hats are available everywhere. For shopping and sightseeing, bring walking shorts, jeans, T-shirts, long-sleeve cotton shirts, slacks, and sundresses. Nighttime dress can range from very informal to casually elegant, depending on the establishment. A tie is practically never required, but a jacket may be appropriate in fancy restaurants. You may need a light sweater or jacket for evening.

▌ PASSPORTS AND VISAS

A valid passport is required to enter or reenter the United States from Aruba.

■ RESTROOMS

Outside of Oranjestad, the only public restrooms you'll find will be in the few restaurants that dot the countryside.

Find a Loo **The Bathroom Diaries** (⊕ *www.thebathroomdiaries.com*) is flush with unsanitized info on restrooms the world over—each one located, reviewed, and rated.

■ SAFETY

Arubans are very friendly, so you needn't be afraid to stop and ask anyone for directions. It's a relatively safe island, but commonsense rules still apply. Lock your rental car when you leave it, and leave valuables in your hotel safe. Don't leave bags unattended in the airport, on the beach, or on tour vehicles.

■TIP→ Distribute your cash, credit cards, IDs, and other valuables between a deep front pocket, an inside jacket or vest pocket, and a hidden money pouch. Don't reach for the money pouch once you're in public.

Contact **Transportation Security Administration** (*TSA* ⊕ *www.tsa.gov*).

■ TAXES

The airport departure tax is $37 for flights to the United States and $33.50 to other destinations, but the fee is usually included in your ticket price. Children under two don't pay departure tax. For purchases you'll pay a 3% BBO tax (a turnover tax on each level of sale for all goods and services) in all but the duty-free shops.

■ TIME

Aruba is in the Atlantic standard time zone, which is one hour later than eastern standard time or four hours earlier than Greenwich mean time. During daylight saving time, between April and October, Atlantic standard is the same time as eastern daylight time.

Time Zones **Timeanddate.com** (⊕ *www.timeanddate.com/world clock*).

■ TIPPING

Restaurants generally include a 10%–15% service charge on the bill; when in doubt, ask. If service isn't included, a 10% tip is standard; if it's included, it's still customary to add something extra, usually small change, at your discretion. Taxi drivers expect a 10%–15% tip, but it isn't mandatory. Porters and bellhops should receive about $2 per bag; chambermaids about $2 a day, but check to see if their tips are included in your bill so you don't overpay.

■ TOURS

You can see the main sights in one day, but set aside two days to really meander. Guided tours are your best option if you have only a short time.

TOUR OPERATORS

De Palm Tours has a near monopoly on Aruban sightseeing; you can make reservations through its general office or at hotel tour-desk branches. The company's basic 4½-hour tour hits the highlights. Wear tennis or hiking shoes, and bring a lightweight jacket or wrap (the air-conditioned bus gets cold). It begins at 9:30 AM, picks you up in your hotel lobby, and costs $75 per person. A full-day Jeep Adventure tour ($130 per person) takes you to sights that would be difficult for you to find on your own and includes a stop at De Palm Island for a little fun in the water. Bring a bandanna to cover your mouth; the ride on rocky dirt roads can get dusty. Prices include round-trip airfare, transfers, sightseeing, and lunch; there's free time for shopping.

Romantic horse-drawn-carriage rides through the city streets of Oranjestad run $40 for a 30-minute tour; hours of operation are 7 PM to 11 PM, and carriages depart from the clock tower at the Royal Plaza Mall.

Contacts **Aruba's Transfer Tour & Taxi** (✉ *Pos Abao 41, Oranjestad* ☎ *297/582-2116*). **De Palm Tours** (✉ *L. G. Smith Blvd. 142, Oranjestad* ☎ *297/582-4400 or 800/766-6016* ⊕ *www.depalm.com*).

SPECIAL-INTEREST TOURS

BOATING

If you try a cruise around the island, know that the choppy waters are stirred up by trade winds and that catamarans are much smoother than single-hulled boats. Sucking on a peppermint or lemon candy may help a queasy stomach; avoid boating with an empty or overly full stomach. Moonlight cruises cost about $40 per person. There are also snorkeling, dinner and dancing, and sunset party cruises to choose from, priced from $40 to $70 per person. Many of the

smaller operators work out of their homes; they often offer to pick you up (and drop you off) at your hotel or meet you at a particular hotel pier.

Contacts **De Palm Tours** (✉ *L. G. Smith Blvd. 142, Oranjestad* ☎ *297/582-4400 or 800/766-6016* ⊕ *www.depalm.com*). **Pelican Tours & Watersports** (✉ *J. E. Irausquin Blvd. 232, Oranjestad* ☎ *297/587-2302* ⊕ *www.pelican-aruba.com*). **Red Sail Sports** (✉ *Renaissance Mall, L. G. Smith Blvd. 82, Oranjestad* ☎ *297/586-1603, 877/733-7245 in U.S.* ⊕ *www.aruba-redsail.com*). **Seaworld Explorer** (☎ *297/586-2416*).

SUBMARINE TOURS

Explore an underwater reef teeming with marine life without getting wet. Atlantis Submarines operates a 65-foot air-conditioned sub that takes 48 passengers 95 to 150 feet below the surface along Barcadera Reef. The two-hour trip (including boat transfer to the submarine platform and 50-minute plunge) costs $99. Make reservations one day in advance. Another option is the *Seaworld Explorer,* a semisubmersible also operated by Atlantis Submarines that allows you to view Aruba's marine habitat from 6 feet below the surface. The cost is $44 for a 1½-hour tour.

Contacts **Atlantis Submarines** (✉ *Renaissance Marina* ☎ *297/583-6090*).

▌ TRIP INSURANCE

Comprehensive travel policies typically cover trip-cancellation and interruption, letting you cancel or cut your trip short because of a personal emergency, illness, or, in some cases, acts of terrorism in your destination. Such policies also cover evacuation and medical care. Some also cover you for trip delays because of bad weather or mechanical problems as well as for lost or delayed baggage. Another type of coverage to look for is financial default—that is, when your trip is disrupted because a tour operator, airline, or cruise line goes out of business. Generally you must buy this when you book your trip or shortly thereafter, and it's only available to you if your operator isn't on a list of excluded companies.

At the very least, consider buying medical-only coverage. Neither Medicare nor some private insurers cover medical expenses anywhere outside of the United States (including time aboard a cruise ship, even if it leaves from a U.S. port). Medical-only policies typically reimburse you for medical care (excluding that related to preexisting conditions) and hospitalization abroad, and provide for evacuation. You still have to pay the bills and await reimbursement from the insurer, though.

Another option is to sign up with a medical-evacuation assistance company. A membership in one of these companies gets you doctor referrals, emergency evacuation or repatriation, 24-hour hotlines for medical consultation, and other assistance. International SOS Assistance Emergency and AirMed International provide evacuation services and medical referrals. MedjetAssist offers medical evacuation.

Expect comprehensive travel insurance policies to cost about 4% to 7% or 8% of the total price of your trip (it's more like 8%–12% if you're over age 70). A medical-only policy may or may not be cheaper than a comprehensive policy. Always read the fine print of your policy to make sure that you are covered for the risks that are of most concern to you. Compare several policies to make sure you're getting the best price and range of coverage available.

▌TIP➔ OK. You know you can save a bundle on trips to warm-weather destinations by traveling in rainy season. But there's also a chance that a severe storm will disrupt your plans. The solution? Look for hotels and resorts that offer storm/hurricane guarantees. Although they rarely allow refunds, most guarantees do let you rebook later if a storm strikes.

Insurance Comparison Sites In-sure My Trip.com (☎800/487–4722 ⊕www.insuremytrip.com). **Square Mouth.com** (☎800/240–0369 or 727/490–5803 ⊕www.squaremouth.com).

Medical Assistance Companies AirMed International Medical Group (⊕www.airmed.com) **International SOS** (⊕www.internationalsos.com). **MedjetAssist** (⊕www.medjetassist.com).

Medical-Only Insurers International Medical Group (☎ 800/628–4664 ⊕ www.im global.com). **Wallach & Company** (☎ 800/237–6615 or 540/687–3166 ⊕ www.wallach.com).

Comprehensive Travel Insurers **Access America** (☎ 866/729–6021 ⊕ www.accessamerica.com). **AIG Travel Guard** (☎ 800/826–4919 ⊕ www.travelguard.com). **CSA Travel Protection** (☎ 800/873–9855 ⊕ www.csatravelprotection.com). **HTH Worldwide** (☎ 610/254–8700 ⊕ www.hthworldwide.com). **Travelex Insurance** (☎ 888/228–9792 ⊕ www.travelex-insurance.com). **Travel Insured International** (☎ 800/243–3174 ⊕ www.travel insured.com).

▌ VISITOR INFORMATION

Before leaving home, contact the Aruba Tourism Authority at one of its many offices. On Aruba the tourist office has free brochures and information officers who are ready to answer any questions you may have, weekdays 7:30 AM–4:30 PM.

The Caribbean Tourism Organization, which has information on the island, is another good resource.

Aruba Information **Aruba Tourism Authority** (☎ 800/862–7822 in the U.S., 297/582–3777 in Aruba ⊕ www.aruba.com).

▌ WEDDINGS

People over the age of 18 can marry as long as they submit the appropriate documents 14 days in advance. Couples are required to submit birth certificates with raised

seals, through the mail or in person, to Aruba's Office of the Civil Registry. They also need an apostil—a document proving they are free to marry—from their country of residence.

With so many beautiful spots to choose from, weddings on Aruba are guaranteed to be romantic. And be sure to register for the island's "One Cool Honeymoon" program for special discounts from local businesses. Ask your hotel for more information.

Aruba Weddings for You is a small company that helps couples make wedding arrangements in advance. Services include securing a location on the island, submitting legal documents, confirming arrangements with suppliers, decorating the venue, and coordinating the ceremony. You can also check out **Aruba Fairy Tales,** another company that arranges weddings.

Information **Aruba Fairy Tales** (✉ Box 4151, Noord ☎ 297/993–0045 🖨 297/583–1511 ⊕ www.aruba fairytales.com). **Aruba Weddings for You** (✉ Nune 92, Paradera ☎ 297/583–7638 🖨 297/588–6073 ⊕ www.arubaweddingsforyou.com).

INDEX